The Day Between
A Memoir of Miracles

by
Abigail Wilson

Printed in the United States of America

First Printing, 2017

ISBN 978-0-9993333-0-3

www.abigailwilsonauthor.com

CreateSpace, a DBA of On-Demand Publishing, LLC

Dedication

I cannot imagine what it would be like to lose a child I'd touched and held and loved in person for seven months. Or 12 years. Or 25 years. Along with giving me just enough grace to endure my pain, the Lord gave me just enough empathy to feel at least a tiny bit of every mother's loss. It was a gift that hurt, but still a gift. ~Page 49

Those were not arbitrary years that I wrote. They referred to very specific mothers and the ages of the children they lost: Jennifer, Jane, Trina.

Jennifer, you were one of the first people that came to mind as I was gripped with our hard news. While I had known of Evan's death when he was just seven months old, it wasn't until I was trying to deal with my own grief that I saw how little I had really understood about your loss. In fact, I began to understand that you may never fully grasp someone else's tragedy, but you can honor it. Trina, you lost your son, Justin, in a car accident, when my sorrow was still so fresh I could taste your pain. In that coming year, your honesty as you shared your grief mirrored a lot of my own. Jane, I felt the passing of sweet KJ so deeply even though I had only known him for such a short amount of time. I couldn't even fathom your sorrow, and yet you were such a testimony of endurance in Christ.

So it was, as I began to write this book, I had to often take out my own grief and hold it and examine it closely so I could write about it. Sometimes the weight of it was too much. But I found that it was your stories, your sons, your own brave journeys forward out of your loss, that helped keep me going when it seemed too hard to go to those dark places. As I cried for my own baby girl, I cried for you. I cried for your sons. In sharing my story, my own journey with grief and hope and death and life, I hope that I honor you and the battles you have fought. I hope I am able to honor your sons who left voids too big to go unnoticed. For Evan, Justin and KJ, I write this book for them. I write it for you. And for all those Abigails, Jennifers, Trinas and Janes, know that you, too, are not alone in your grief. Not only do we have each other, but we also have a Father in heaven who has experienced that same loss of a Son.

To all the mommies who have lost your babies: This book is for you.

Prologue

I sat on the hard plastic chair in the emergency room trying to decide if I was feeling any cramps. I knew I was bleeding, but I didn't know if it was serious. What was on that scary list of miscarriage signs doctors give you? Where was WebMD when I needed it? When I called my husband at work to tell him I was bleeding, I tried to channel calmness into the phone – calmness I didn't feel. It wasn't a lot of blood, but when you're pregnant any bleeding is ridiculously scary. I was not calm. I had only recently learned I was pregnant. I barely had my mind wrapped around the idea of having another baby, and I was now suddenly in fear of losing it.

When Brett walked through the door, I felt a rush of relief followed immediately by guilt. As an infantry officer in the U.S. Army, Brett was always on duty. Leaving in the middle of a workday showed just how serious this whole thing was. Thankfully, we were soon ushered back into a little room for an ultrasound. At only eight weeks along, there wasn't much else to do. We waited for what seemed like an eternity while the ER doctor looked for a heartbeat. And there it was, a little heart beating away. The army doctor bluntly informed me to not get too excited. I might still be in the process of having a miscarriage, and this early in the game, there was nothing they could do about it. He said a comparison between blood tests that day and again four days later would show whether my hormone levels had doubled as they should. Only after that would we know if all was well with my pregnancy. Until then we'd just have to wait it out.

This doctor was about as gentle as a meat cleaver. I left feeling both tentatively relieved that the baby still had a heartbeat, but I was also beyond scared. I had never felt so completely out of control. I stared down at the ultrasound picture they handed me. It was a little white blob inside a giant black hole. At eight weeks babies are teeny, but they are still babies. Hearing that heartbeat had made me fall so very much in love with whomever had taken up residence in my uterus. I wanted so very badly for that baby in there to be okay. So began a four-day prayer and waiting spree.

I hate waiting, and I know I'm not alone in that. Nobody likes it because it reminds us we are not in control. Whoever doesn't have to wait has the upper hand. This is why doctors, DMV employees, and internet repairmen are so powerful. Anyone who can make me wait half a day and then bill me for it, those are the people with real control. In this case, time was in control, and I knew that it was God who was ultimately in control. So I prayed my little heart out. I pled with Him to tell me everything would be okay, that all was not lost, that this baby would live. Through all the prayers and tears He reminded me of His truth. It was something I had written the year before around Easter:

> The other night when I was reading poetry, I came across a gem that I've been pondering for the past few days. I've been thinking about what comes after Good Friday. The horror of that day is true and real, and I shudder when I think about my Christ upon that hill, dying for me. But I kind of brushed over the whole "three days" aspect. I brushed over Saturday and right on into Easter - right up to that empty tomb.
>
> But today I'm stuck on Saturday. Twenty-four hours of nothing. Twenty-four hours of Sabbath. For the disciples, for those followers of Jesus who loved Him and hoped in Him, Sabbath would have meant a day of rest - a day to reflect. So there they were, their Hope had just died, and they were forced to sit and do nothing. Doing nothing is the worst kind of awfulness, in my opinion.
>
> I've always liked that it was the women who went to Jesus' tomb on Sunday morning, as the sun rose and the Sabbath was over, but now I'm looking at it differently. I'm thinking of them on Saturday, and how they must have sat together searching their minds for the meaning of this awful act. How they talked together about what to do next - how to move on. How they must have wanted to do something. But I think it was no accident that our Lord died on a Friday; that those whom He loved would have to wait a day. Sit and wait with nothing to do.

When things do not go my way, I often expect that tomorrow will bring the answer, that tomorrow things will be set aright. But what if it doesn't? What if tomorrow things are not all right? What if we are asked instead to sit still?

I suppose it's there that I have an advantage over those first followers of Jesus. I know what happens on Sunday. I know how the new week begins. I hope when I am asked to sit quietly on my "day in between," I will do so with a little more faith knowing that Easter will come. Salvation will arise. Light will triumph over darkness. I hope I'll remember that sometimes I must be still and quiet and be faithful in my waiting.

Happy Good Saturday, my friends. As we sit and wait for Sunday, may we remember that in all of our darkness, Easter is coming.

I was greatly encouraged by this reminder: Sometimes it is not for me to act, but instead to sit and wait. This lesson would encompass the very essence of my whole pregnancy for me. As our family walked through our own "Day Between," as we faced both death and life, despair and hope, we would come to see there was so much to learn from all that came between. At the time I re-read this journal entry, I thought it was just a little comfort for the three days I had to wait before I could go back to the doctor. Isn't that often how it is? The Lord softly speaks, and we rush through it and say, "Yeah, yeah! I get it!" When really, we have barely scratched the surface.

That was the Day Between the Night Before-
The blood
still wet upon the hill;
His body
wrapped.
entombed,
and still;
the great stone sealed
with Roman seal
and guarded well.
Many a Judean home
had now become
a lesser tomb
within whose walls
men lay,
whose Life had died
That Day.

Looking back
we cannot share
their black
despair.
For us
He is the Risen Christ,
as He had said:
for them, that Shabbat,
all life died--
for He was dead.
That was the Day Between the Night Before.
This is my Day Between, my Night Before...
Suspended
in this interim-
let me be still,
let me adore,
let me remember
Him.
*~Ruth Graham Bell**

* Sitting By My Laughing Fire, by Ruth Bell Graham, © 1977, The Ruth Graham Literacy Trust, used by permission, all rights reserved.

The Day Between

Chapter One

Our lives were about to be changed forever. I would no longer live a day without the ache in my heart where death had left its mark. I would no longer see life without thinking what it had cost. What I would learn from those ten months would be etched upon my heart, and it would overflow into how I saw Jesus and how I saw myself. But, as it is with most life-altering events, we had no warning our lives were about to be turned upside down.

Maybe once I start looking back to scrutinize my day-to-day for any warning signs, I might remember that time I saw a Doublemint gum commercial with the twin girls running through a field of daisies, and realize that it had been a direct message that I would one day be pregnant with twin girls. Or not.

In reality our lives continued in the normal routine—as normal as a military family can be, anyway—right up until the moment we left normal behind. I'd say we looked very average and unexciting from the outside: Soldier husband, wife, young son.

Brett and I met in high school. He was a super serious, geeky guy with enviably curly hair, and I was a high-spirited—for lack of a nicer word—sarcastic drama queen who didn't have *time* to be serious. I never would have dreamed that four years after high school, after we'd both graduated college and grown up a lot, we would end up at the same New Year's Eve party in our hometown. That we would start chatting and (insert really fast courtship and engagement here) end up getting married. Nope. Would not have guessed. But we did.

Sure, I understood pretty much *nothing* about military life, and sure, my husband says about half as many words as I do, at about one third the speed in any given day, but we have the really important things in common. Namely, Jesus.

When we began dating, Brett was already in the army, so courtship for us required phone communication and letters. Yes, real letters. The circumstances of military life sometimes require snail mail even in the twenty-first century. When Brett was in Ranger School, letters were our primary communication. Sometimes the words would just fall off the page where he had fallen asleep while writing, yet I treasured every scribble.

After having many long-distance phone conversations and sending some pretty hefty letters back and forth, Brett and I finally sat down to have what I *knew* was the inevitable "talk," wherein he would wax eloquent about how perfect we were for each other, and how he wanted to start dating. But that's not how it went *at all.*

I was living by myself in a tiny garage apartment – the single girl dream – and there was this guy in my living room at 9:30 at night. I was sure he was ready to profess his love, but instead it went like this:

> "I should not be here."
> "Um. OK?"
> "It is highly inappropriate for me to be here alone in your house late at night."
> "Well, can we make an exception?"
> "Okay - this once."

I figured this was a good sign, since I was still holding out hope for the whole Austentonian love confession. Brett rushed forward with his clearly rehearsed speech.

> "You should know I am probably not going to have a typical life. I feel really strongly about having people live in my house with whom I can help in their relationship with Jesus. If that's too much for you, then how I feel about you won't really matter."

I'll stop here, dear reader, so you can all catch your breath after the steaminess of his opening line. But seriously, it *was* one of the most romantic things anyone could have said to me, because I had been *praying* and *dreaming* of a guy who would put his relationship with Christ and his calling from the Lord above his feelings for me. Be still my heart. Even better, I actually had hoped and dreamed to one day have a house that was open for one and all to come. For people to stay, any length of time- to give them time to grow, heal, and hear from the Lord. As unromantic as it may sound, I pretty much would have married Brett right then and there. It didn't happen quite so quickly, but we did indeed get married soon afterwards, and I headed into the crazy and mind-bending world of military wifedom.

This episode may seem like it has little to do with this story, but the army certainly plays its own special role in our lives. The best way to sum up what it is to be the wife of an army infantry officer, is to describe my husband's job like a super toxic friend. I cannot control her. She can call him up and demand his presence for any length of time, at any hour of the day or night. Hours. Days. Months. Longer. She is constantly lying and betraying by telling us one thing and doing the exact opposite when we least expect it. She's not all bad, because she also sends us on some mighty exciting adventures together, making us grow beyond ourselves by asking us to do things we never thought possible. So, no, she's not *all bad*. But she's definitely a constant presence - defining a heavy chunk of our identity, whether we like her every day or not. She is most pushy and overbearing during and after deployment. When Brett deployed for a year, we had to reacquaint ourselves with the long distance relationship of our dating season. But, she backed off a bit when Brett got back from deployment and was in a training school for six months. During that interlude of her mercy, I got pregnant with our son, Ransom.

We were stationed at Fort Benning, near Columbus, Georgia, when Ransom was born. Ransom, let's just say, was not the easiest of babies. He was high maintenance, colicky, and adorable, with his head full of hair, those chunky, kissable cheeks, and intense stare like his daddy's. But I earned my mommy stripes his first year of life. Being the doer I am, during my pregnancy I read every baby book I could get my hands on. When Ransom was born, I was ready. I returned any curve ball Ransom could throw at me with my own special type-A brand of parenting. A tight and rigid nap schedule and a highly regulated diet of homemade organic baby food were my answers to any problem. I even single-parented the first two months while Brett was in an army school. Yup, I figured I had learned everything I ever needed to know about mommyhood, and I wore my accomplishments proudly - probably *too* proudly.

The first six months of 2012 were pretty standard for a young military family. Brett was gone for two months in training, Ransom was growing and learning, and life was moving right along. The year before, just as we were settling into our life in Georgia, Brett felt like God told him to pursue an assignment to San Antonio, Texas. We had good friends moving there, and Brett felt God wanted us to learn and grow from their example as followers of Christ. The likelihood of the army sending us to San Antonio seemed slim. The post there doesn't specialize in Brett's field of expertise. Also, we knew Brett would first have to complete his current assignment at Fort Benning. Even though it was another year or two away, I was already preparing myself for the inevitable: If we wanted to move to San Antonio, Brett would probably have to get out of the army and find another job.

Although the routine seemed pretty calm at the time, I expected faith-stretching times ahead. I was already thinking about scheduling some time to start *pre*-worrying about that seemingly inevitable job change ahead. I've always been one to get a head start when it comes to worry. Yet, even with that on my agenda, we lived and walked and breathed and grew in the early months of 2012. We didn't know what was coming around the bend for us until it arrived with little fanfare. Isn't that always how truly life-changing seasons usually enter? Without warning everything turns upside down. With our story, everything changed with a trip to the bathroom. Yes, the bathroom which is the most dramatic setting for all the juiciest stories.

Chapter Two

Following a long night of eight hours of sleep and an exhausting Saturday morning of doing absolutely nothing, I was taking a nap on the couch. And I really needed that nap. I also really needed to pee. My body was clearly telling me something, so I took a pregnancy test. Two birds, one stone: I needed to pee, and I needed to know if my hunch was legit.

I came back from the bathroom and calmly sat down on the couch next to Brett, who had no clue how much our life had just changed. And I didn't tell him. I sat there for a whole hour. For some reason it's really hard for me to break pregnancy news. It's just *such* big news, and I feel like balloons and confetti should be involved. But I'm a terrible balloon-blower-upper, and confetti is impossible to clean up. So I just sat on the news until we went for a walk around the neighborhood, pushing not-yet-two-year-old Ransom in the stroller. Finally, the news was too much to handle, and I awkwardly blurted it out. Brett was surprised and excited, and we circled the block a few times discussing logistics. Yes, logistics. Army, remember?

Because of Brett's job, things, dinner, vacations, having babies, are not always easy to plan. So many military wife friends of mine have had babies without their husbands by their side because of deployment, training, or some other army business. I did not want to be one of those women, but I knew it was possible Brett would be deployed when this baby was born. We did some military-life math and figured my due date was sometime at the beginning of January 2013. Sure enough, chances were good Brett would be deployed. I immediately started to freak out about this possibility and spent my nights worrying about having a baby and raising two children alone. All kinds of things freak me out. I generally do not do well with unknowns. I find safety and security in control, absolutes, black and white. Having a baby during deployment is none of those things.

Granted, my worries were about major events—giving birth without Brett, knowing he could be deployed to a dangerous place—but none of it was happening to us yet. Still, I was primed and ready to worry. As usual, I had a plan. I tried to conquer all my fears with a plan, with tasks for me to control and do. But in spite of all my plans and fears, something far, far different happened; something so difficult I could never have prepared for it even if I had known it was coming.

This verse comes to mind:

> *The heart of man plans his way, but the Lord establishes his steps.*
> *Proverbs 16:9 (ESV)*

There we were, circling the block, making our contingency plans, while the Lord was making a path. A path that would lead to unfathomable blessing and sorrow, a path, that—as they always do—would lead us to Him.

Not long after I found out I was pregnant, my trip to the ER for bleeding gave me a good ol' fashioned reality check. I should have taken the hint I was going to have plenty to worry about without any imaginary "what if" scenarios. Realizing I could be having a miscarriage, and I couldn't do anything to stop it, was a nightmare. However, along with the wonderful word the Lord gave me regarding Easter and the season of waiting, He also laid another verse on my heart:

> *Kings will be your children's guardians, their princesses will nurse your*
> *children... Then you will recognize that I am the Lord; those who wait*
> *patiently for me are not put to shame. Isaiah 49:23 (NET)*

This verse was confusing to me, but it mentioned children and patience which was clearly the message of the day. It didn't make much sense to me otherwise, but I knew in my heart it was meant for me. And, as it is with all words from the Lord, even when we don't fully understand them, it brought an unexplainable peace to my heart when I read it.

After four days of waiting and praying, we were feeling

positive as we went to my follow-up appointment. I hadn't had any more bleeding, and I was feeling more and more nauseated by the day - all good signs. I felt so confident that I told Brett not to worry about coming to the doctor with me. As I mentioned, his job was pretty high stress and taking time off was always a challenge. So I put on my big-girl-army-wife panties and headed off to the doctor for the follow-up ultrasound alone.

Having an actual obstetrician and not Dr. Meat Cleaver examine me made me feel more calm, like everything was under control. Everything was going to be.... *Wait. What's that?*

The army OB doctor had been sliding her ultra sound wand around checking on the baby, who had a heartbeat, hooray! Then her little wand found another heartbeat. Another baby. A second whole little person with its own little heartbeat. I was having twins. *Pinch me! I must be dreaming!*

I've always thought that was just a silly statement people say. I mean, seriously, who doesn't know when they're awake or sleeping? But when I saw those two babies on the ultrasound screen, my mind revolted. Could this be even remotely reality? No way. Therefore, I must be having some sort of waking dream.

Even though clearly there were two little bodies and two little heartbeats, the doctor ran to get a second opinion to make sure she was right. Apparently she couldn't believe it either. While

I waited, I simultaneously cried and looked for the hidden cameras. I had just been told I was going to have twins: I absolutely *had to* cry, and at the same time I could only imagine someone must be playing an elaborate prank on me. I then followed this up with some healthy praying in which I told God this was all very funny, but I could not handle twins.

There is an utterly false phrase commonly used, even among Christians, which I think hurts and confuses people. "God doesn't give you more than you can handle." For me those words bring doubt instead of reassurance, because if God thinks I can handle twins, then He must not know me *at all*. He must have me confused with that super-with-it chick down the street.

But when you look through the Bible to find examples of this platitude, you will find the Bible is stock full of examples of people in situations far above what they can handle. I'm pretty sure Abraham and Sarah were not really up for chasing after a toddler in their triple digits. Joseph probably couldn't handle being left for dead in a pit and then stuck in prison for something he didn't do. Moses straight-up told God he could not handle being the leader of an entire nation of people. Joshua probably knew he couldn't handle the task of defeating all the nations living in God's promised land. Esther probably wasn't down with being the queen to a scary king of the known world and then having to stand up to this scary king as an advocate for her people. If we could do interviews with these biblical figures, I'm sure they would say something like, "I totally couldn't handle it." The good news is God *can* handle it - all of it.

Based on my life experiences so far, I believe God is constantly placing me in situations I can't handle. He doesn't do this out of spite or meanness. He does it because He loves me. He wants to give me the opportunity to learn He can handle what I can't. Turns out I can't handle much, so I get daily lessons on the awesome power of God. He has to help me get out of bed, have patience with my toddler, think of others before myself and on and on. Then once in a great while, someone delivers a piece of news like, "You're having twins." For God this is like a "Let-me-show-you-what-I-can-do" Christmas. He doesn't stop at the daily stuff I can't handle. No, God wants to bring out the big guns, to show me how big and awesome and powerful He truly is.

So, yes, I was having twins, and no, I couldn't handle it.

Chapter Three

When I recovered from the initial shock of the news about our twins, I began to get excited. For one thing, there is *nothing* more fun than breaking the news about having twins. It's entertaining every time. Given my flair for the dramatic, I loved to casually drop the news into a conversation and watch for the reaction of shock and awe.

I texted the ultrasound picture of our two little beans to several close friends and family. No words, just the image. Then I sat by my phone like a giddy little girl on Christmas morning, just waiting for them to call. And call they did, because no one can respond to a picture like that with a plain old text message. Except my mother, who apparently couldn't see the plain-as-day two babies. She simply responded, "Cute." Cute? I thought, "Wow. Mom is clearly more levelheaded than I imagined.

Apparently having twin grandchildren is just no big deal to her!" Later in the day she talked to my dad and realized what she had overlooked and immediately called me. It was the best! It was like throwing a bunch of little surprise parties, one right after the other.

Having twins was definitely special. Even though multiple births, including fraternal twins have increased in recent years, twins still make up only 3 percent of all pregnancies. Brett and I beat the odds by conceiving twins, especially since we weren't in high-probability categories like using fertility treatments, having twins in our family history, or being over 35 in age. But there was still more to come for our odds-defying pregnancy.

Most twins are fraternal, formed by two separately fertilized eggs. Identical twins are formed when one fertilized egg splits into two. Identical twins are even more rare, about 4 out of every 1,000 pregnancies or .4%. Don't overlook the decimal there. That's point four percent of all pregnancies. Early ultrasounds indicated our twins were indeed identical, so we rocked that percentage too.

I discovered all these probabilities through very scientific methods, i.e. a massive Google search. More internet cramming taught me that after an egg is fertilized, development begins quickly. In the case of identical twins, if the egg splits before the amniotic sacs are fully developed, the mother's body knows it has two babies, so it makes two amniotic sacs. Sometimes this does not happen, and identical twins may share one amniotic sac. Placental development is similar. If the egg splits before the placenta develops, then the mother's body will form two, one for each baby. If the mother's body has already created the placenta, which is the source of nourishment for the baby, then oops, too late, there's only going to be one placenta to go around. Identical twins may share an amniotic sac, a placenta, or both. Or neither.

Let's stop here and just marvel at science. I mean, I know I'm an English major, and I only understand a teeny tiny speck of what some people understand about life, but to me, this intricacy points to one thing: There is a God.

In the early weeks of my pregnancy, doctors couldn't tell if our twins were sharing an amniotic sac and a placenta, or if they each had their own. They were finally able to distinguish two sacs, but let me tell you, those suckers are hard to see on an ultrasound. Further ultrasounds revealed our twins were probably sharing a placenta. Apparently, on the day my body was handing out placentas, we still had only one baby; so one placenta was all we got.

This is when our doctors first mentioned twin-to-twin transfusion syndrome, or TTTS, which affects 15 percent of identical twins. Our doctor explained when babies share a placenta, there is a chance they won't be able to share it equally. If twins develop TTTS, one becomes the donor twin, receiving less blood flow and nutrients. The other, the recipient twin, receives more blood flow and nutrients. The donor risks dehydration and lack of development - in short starvation. While the recipient twin may be overwhelmed by fluid, its body may not handle the excess. In other words, TTTS would put both our babies in danger.

At the time we were optimistic about everything, so when they told us our babies were probably sharing a placenta, I thought, *But look how hard it was to see the two amniotic sacs! I mean, everything is majorly microscopic in there. I bet they just can't see the other placenta.* As for this twin-to-twin business and its 15 percent likelihood, I was happy to push that to the back of my brain as a remote possibility. After all, the twins had an 85% of *not* developing TTTS. The math was a comfort to me. That was the first—and probably the only—time I will ever take comfort in math. Since we've talked about science from an English major's point of view, let's move on to math as a way to further illustrate the miraculous phenomenon of our odds-defying babies.

On second thought, I couldn't even begin to figure the percentages that got us to this point. What is 15 percent of .4 percent of 3 percent anyway? Is that even a number? The hard math I didn't want to know then, but learned later, was that TTTS occurs in about .1 percent of pregnancies - one in a thousand.

It was clear these babies were something very special from the Lord, but their condition was less clear for several months. We were left with a lot of "what ifs," and "wait and sees." The internet was kind enough to spout out numbers to cling to when I wondered things like, "what are the *odds?*" Unfortunately, the internet also spewed some horrible statistics involving what could happen as our pregnancy continued. I could not always convince myself those odds were in our favor. The months ticked by, and every visit with the doctor was punctuated with another "wait and see." In all the waiting, even when the math couldn't reassure me, God did. I knew He could defy the odds when we couldn't. He defied the odds to give us these babies, so I knew they belonged to Him. He could, and would, take care of them.

During this "wait and see" period, a family friend pulled some strings to obtain an ultrasound to determine the sex of the babies a few weeks earlier than scheduled. While we were visiting family in Texas, Brett, my mom, and my sister, Anna, went with me to the ultrasound appointment. A part of me was still half hopeful our doctors were mistaken. If this ultrasound showed one was a boy and the other a girl, we would know they were not identical, and we could stop worrying about all the awful possibilities. We were filled with all kinds of butterflies and last minute bets until we saw them on the screen: our perfect little girls. We still couldn't see whether they were sharing a placenta, and our friend, the ultrasound tech, said even the amniotic sacs were difficult to make out. But girl parts? Those were clear.

Brett didn't say anything for a solid twenty minutes. Later, when I asked him about it, he said he felt such an overwhelming sense of responsibility and love for the girls, he immediately started planning out how to murder their prom dates and hide the bodies. Daddy stuff like that. He also mentioned he had an overwhelming desire for a stiff drink.

My mom and Anna were mostly in shock about seeing the twins on the ultrasound. It is an incredible thing to witness. I was stunned to know we were having *girls*. For the record I would have been stunned by having boys too. The kicker was not the gender, but the "s" at the end of those words. Girls. Plural.

We were one step more in love with our girls. What a lovely thing to say! I reveled in saying it: Our girls would be born in the winter. Our girls would need lots of cute clothes. Good thing our girls had two girl cousins who share. *Our girls, our girls, our girls.* So even though there was still much to worry about, I started to plan, and to hope, and to dream.

Back at home in Georgia after our Texas vacation, we faced more serious discoveries as my pregnancy progressed. The girls—with their two amniotic sacs and one placenta—became more clear in every ultrasound. Our doctors talked less and less about the possibility of TTTS and more and more about the severity of TTTS in the babies. It's all a bit of a blur. I know we worried (a lot), went to doctor's appointments (many), but we definitely did not talk enough about the TTTS and how serious it really was.

This part is hard to recount, because when I look back on it with hindsight, it dredges up so many what-ifs. What if I had known more, done something sooner, asked for more advice, or gone to different doctors? Yet, this is all part of the lesson that comes from the day between - from a forced upon day of rest. Those words from my blog post way back at the beginning of our story seemingly whispered in my ear: The disciples had to, *"Sit and wait with nothing to do."* And this was our own time of waiting instead of a time of action. When Brett and I talk about this particular part of our journey, we always come back to this: Even in those days of uncertainty, the Lord was in charge. It's easy to believe God is working when His movements are visible. But what about the days, weeks, or months when His hand is not apparent? Can I believe the Lord is present in those times too?

This reminded me of the Bible story in the Gospel of John chapter 11, when Jesus heard His friend Lazarus was sick. It says that because Jesus loved Mary and Martha (Lazarus' sisters), he waited for two days before going to Lazarus' house. Can you imagine how the sisters felt? They send a message to Jesus letting him know that Lazarus is really sick and instead of Him rushing over like they imagined He would, He seems to inexplicably do nothing! But it was because Jesus loved them that He waited. How powerful to think that seeming apathy could actually be an act of the Lord's love on our behalf. When Jesus finally got to Lazarus' house, it was obviously too late, at least by human standards. Lazarus had been dead for days. His sisters took turns telling Jesus, "If you had been here, my brother would not have died." They had had faith in Jesus' power, but not in His timing. During their days of waiting, Mary and Martha could not see Jesus' plan. They prayed for healing that didn't come. While all along Jesus had a more remarkable miracle in mind. He called Lazarus out of the tomb and raised him from the dead.

It is hard for a chronic doer like myself to remember that God's timing is essential to His plan. Waiting for His timing may even feel like neglectfulness to us, only because we can't always see what He is doing. We would be satisfied with a small miracle now, just because it would show action on God's part. But His plan is, instead, to wait and reveal even more of His power later. It was hard for our family to wait and to watch our baby girls slip further and further into serious danger. But our time of waiting was a testament to God's love for us. I probably won't understand all the details of how His love was at work until I'm in heaven, but I *do* believe, even in those days of seeming inaction, He was with us.

From the beginning I worried about Baby B and not Baby A. From a purely non-scientific standpoint, it was sobering to see our Baby B on the ultrasound screen. She was curled into the tiniest of balls up in the corner of the picture - hardly moving. She *couldn't* move. It was apparent she had become the donor twin. Because she wasn't getting as much fluid as Baby A, she wasn't passing much fluid to fill the amniotic sac. Who knew amniotic fluid is basically pee? Until this experience, I surely didn't. At the same time, Baby A was receiving and passing tons of fluid, so she had plenty of room to move around. Girlfriend wouldn't stop moving. She was in constant motion, flips, and somersaults. Doing measurements on her was practically impossible. To us, non-medical professionals, a moving baby is a healthy baby, and so I delighted in my little mover. I'm so grateful for the many, many ultrasounds we had at the beginning. I'll never forget those images of my baby girl - moving, moving, moving. I delighted in being the knowing mother when the ultrasound techs would comment on her busy, active ways.

"She's *always* like that!" I'd say.

It was Baby B, curled up and stuck up in the corner of every picture, hardly moving at all, who gave us clues that things were not going to be okay.

My physical condition at the time was another clue, especially in hindsight, that things were not going well. I was blogging through my pregnancy, and I wrote that I felt like I'd gone from my first trimester directly into my third - with ligament pains, Braxton-Hicks contractions, and feeling like a ten-ton gorilla. The extra fluid around Baby A was getting to me. My body knew, even before my brain did, that something was not right. At the beginning of August, I wrote a blog that makes me cry every time I read it. It brings back the physical sensations. My tears are partly sorrow, because now I understand better what my body was trying to tell me. They are also tears of thankfulness, because I understand God heard my cries for help. At the time, I knew nothing, only the fear in my heart. The Lord, on the other hand, knew all. Even then, when I couldn't see it, He was working things out. Here's what I wrote:

> It's 6:15 pm, and I'm on my knees. My top half is draped over a giant green Swiss ball (the best position for my back I've found). I'm in Ransom's room, and he's playing like an angel baby at his window, pushing a little farmer around in a little

tiny tractor.

And I'm balling my eyes out. It's been building up for a while. Who knows why today was hard? I didn't do anything differently on this Monday from any other. A morning walk, library time, lunch, naptime, grocery store. But coming back from the store was hard. My body is so heavy. I get out of breath going up stairs, much less going up and down five times with bags of groceries. That was three hours ago, yet the exhaustion isn't gone. I could barely make dinner and feed Ransom.

For maybe the first time ever I was tempted to call Brett at work and tell him to come home. But what was I going to tell my husband who's been up since 4 a.m.? "I'm tired; come home!"? And seriously, what exactly is so overwhelming? Is it our child, who's been playing by himself for hours now, talking to himself, making up conversations with his animals and little people? Was it dinner that took maybe ten minutes to prepare?

No. I'm crying, because I'm so scared of the future, of tomorrow and the next day. I tell my friends that I'm "so big," and they think I am saying I look fat.
They say, "no, no, no."
Or, "Well you ARE carrying twins."
But that's not what I mean. This has nothing to do with vanity. This has to do with the fact that my back hurts all the time, that it's hard to sleep, and at four and a half months, I look like I did when I was eight months pregnant with Ransom. I'm afraid of what the second half of this pregnancy will bring, and we're talking the BEST-case scenario in which the girls are doing fine. I do not know how I'm going to do this.

And so I kneel, draped over a green Swiss ball, remembering

that kneeling is a very good position to pray in. And I cry out for help, because that's all I can do.

> *I hear, and my body trembles;*
> *my lips quiver at the sound;*
> *rottenness enters into my bones;*
> *my legs tremble beneath me.*
> *Yet I will quietly wait for the day of trouble*
> *to come upon people who invade us.*
>
> *Though the fig tree should not blossom*
> *nor there be fruit on the vines.*
> *the produce of the olive fail*
> *and the fields yield no food,*
> *the flock be cut off from the fold*
> *and there be no herd in the stalls,*
> *yet I will rejoice in the Lord,*
> *I will take joy in the God of my salvation*
> *God, the Lord, is my strength;*
> *he makes my feet like deer;*
> *he makes me tread on my high places.*
> *Habakkuk 3:16-19 (ESV)*

Our days passed. We worried, and we wondered, and my body suffered. Nothing seemed to be happening, other than our girls continued to develop. Baby B was more and more stuck, while Baby A was still swimming around. Yet, something *was* happening. The Lord was about to make a move.

Chapter Four

It was during this time of waiting, God gave us a wonderful gift. He helped us choose special names for our girls. In light of all that came after, this was more important to me than words can say. I believe names are meaningful and important. In Biblical times, a person's name was essentially a prophecy about that person. In fact, names meant enough to God that He sometimes changed a person's name to signify a turning point in their life. So for biblical reasons—also possibly because I'm an English Major nerd who places a big emphasis on words—the naming of our children had the utmost importance to us.

When we found out we were expecting, Brett and I had two names picked out: one for a girl and one for a boy. I mean, that's all we would need, right? Of course, God had other plans, and we needed names for two girls.

God had spoken the name Priscilla into my heart four years before. It was such a clear message from the Lord, that from that point on, I had no doubt we would have a daughter one day, and her name would be Priscilla Beth. In the Bible, a woman named Priscilla and her husband, Aquila, are mentioned quite a few times, showing much about her character. She and her husband worked beside Paul in their trade of tent making and, more importantly, their work of sharing the gospel. At one point, they even risked their lives to save Paul's life. Whether it was hosting a church in her home, teaching, working, or just encouraging others, Priscilla was always helping to strengthen her fellow believers.

My favorite passage about Priscilla and Aquila tells about their encounter with a man named Apollos, who had been teaching about the coming Messiah but didn't know about Jesus. Acts chapter 18 tells how they took the guy aside and said, "Look here! There is so much more to the story!" Afterward, Apollos became a huge asset to the early church in spreading the Good News.

So we named Baby A, our little super swimmer, Priscilla Beth. At the time I thought our prayer for her would play out just as I prayed it and wrote it down for her at the time:

> We pray our own little Priscilla would have the Gospel of Christ written on her life in such a way that she, like Priscilla in the Bible, would find a multitude of ways to help bring Life to others. May she be a teacher and a servant, and may she be an encouragement to others when they are in need.

Her middle name also has great significance to us, because it speaks of two of the most important women in our lives: our own mothers. My mom, Leabeth, and Brett's mom, Mary Elizabeth, are part of the very foundation of our own spiritual—not to mention physical—lives. We are so grateful for the sacrifices they have made to follow the Lord's calling in their own lives. It has been a wonderful example to us. We are so grateful for the prayers they have prayed for us. Those prayers have been the nourishment of our lives. And we pray our own little daughter would one day grow into a woman who can reflect even a little of her grandmothers. They are both women to whom she can proudly look for guidance and council.

For Baby B we chose the name Tabitha Lorien. As soon as we had the name, we knew immediately that it was the perfect name for our little girl. When she was named, she was so tiny, struggling to live and grow, and we wondered how she could ever survive her circumstances. In the Bible there was a woman named Tabitha who was always doing good and serving those around her. But Acts chapter 9 says Tabitha got very sick and died. After she died, all those who loved her and had been the recipients of her love, told Jesus' disciple, Peter, all about her. Peter went up to the room where her body had been laid out. He said, "Tabitha, get up," and she immediately came back to life. The Bible then says that because of this amazing event, many believed in the Lord.

As for her middle name, we make no apologies for its nerdiness. It comes from J.R.R. Tolkien's *The Lord of the Rings*. It is the shortened name of Lothlorien, the land of the elves. In all my years of reading Tolkien's books, the passages describing Lorien have had always been favorites for me. In the context of the story, the struggle of good and evil in a world on the brink of war, Lorien is the perfect picture of heaven. Tolkien described Lorien in this way:

A light was upon it for which his language had no name. All that he saw was shapely, but the shapes seemed at once clear cut, as if they had been first conceived and drawn at the uncovering of his eyes, and ancient as if they had endured forever. He saw no color but those he knew, gold and white and blue and green, but they were fresh and poignant, as if he had at that moment first perceived them and made for them names new and wonderful. In winter here no heart could mourn for summer or for spring. No blemish or sickness or deformity could be seen in anything that grew upon the earth. On the land of Lorien there was no stain. The world is indeed full of peril and in the it there are many dark places, but still there is much that is fair, and though in all lands love is now mingled with grief, Lorien grows perhaps the greater.

This was our prayer for Tabitha when she received her name:

> Our own little Tabitha is so small, and seems to have so much going against her in these early days of her life. It is our prayer that the Lord would indeed bring her back, even from death, so He might be glorified, and that many would believe in Him. In her life, we pray she would have a servant heart like her biblical namesake and her current namesake, our friend Tabitha Trott. Tabitha and I have been friends for a long time, and she is one of those people who is so incredibly solid - so incredibly faithful. I know with all

my heart she will be the same person throughout all my children's lives - serving the Lord, giving her life to Him. She will be an example to our little Tabitha, as a servant-minded disciple of the Lord. We pray our Tabitha Lorien's life will always be grounded in something much greater than herself. She will always know there is something much more wonderful for which to fight. We have our own future—even more glorious than Lorien—to look forward to.

Scripture reassures me these names were decided long before Brett and I knew them.

Before I was born the Lord called me, while I was in my mother's womb, he recorded my name. Isaiah 49:1

So it was with that we went, armed with the God-given names of our daughters, into one of the greatest battles of the pregnancy. Two short weeks later, in the hottest days of August, our concerns about twin-to-twin transfusion became absolutes.

I was seeing Dr. Sheridan, a local fetal specialist weekly, and it was at one of those appointments that our world shifted. It was very difficult for Brett to get away from work to accompany me, especially for such frequent appointments, so I was alone that day. As usual, I had an ultrasound, and saw our little girls. I was uncomfortable as I waited on the hard slab of a table—granted, I wasn't comfortable anywhere at that point—with my shirt pulled up, and my stomach covered in gooey gel. I wish I had bought stock in ultrasound gel. By the end of my pregnancy I had enough of it squeezed onto my stomach to cover a football field in blue, goopy awesomeness. It was a terribly long wait, and all I could do was watch the hands move around the face of the clock above me. The technician hadn't been able to get measurements on Priscilla, who was always moving, so I wondered if that was the reason for the delay.

After an hour of excruciating waiting, the doctor finally came in the room. I could tell immediately that her concern was about more than not getting Priscilla's measurements. The doctor said she believed the girls' condition was serious and only surgery to divide the placenta would give either of them a fighting chance of survival. She said it needed to happen soon. She said she would make the calls to set it up at Texas Children's Hospital in Houston, Texas, one of only three hospitals in the country performing the surgery at the time.

When I got in the car, I cried and cried. Then I tried to call Brett before driving home in a daze. Looking back, it seems crazy how much bad news I got when Brett couldn't be there because of the army. But I am aware that all the times I really needed him, he was right by my side. The Lord was ever faithful.

At that point, neither Brett nor I really understood the urgency of our girls' condition. Since we figured it would take a week or two for the hospital and our insurance company to get their acts together and schedule the surgery, we resigned ourselves that nothing would happen right away.

But to my surprise, on Thursday, just two days after the ultrasound, Texas Children's Hospital called me to begin the process, asking specific questions about my pregnancy and my current symptoms. I told them, among other things, I had been experiencing some cramping. Apparently, some of my answers sent up a red flag, because at 6:30 that same evening Dr. Campbell, my obstetrician, called. She told me to head straight to the civilian hospital in Columbus for observation because it was possible the cramping I had described could be early labor.

Chapter Five

Things were getting real. I knew if I was truly in labor, then taking a trip to have surgery was out of the question. By now, I also knew not having the surgery was a death sentence for both girls. Oh, and when I got this news, Brett was in the field. Once again I was getting bad, scary news all by myself.

"In the field" refers to military training in simulated mission conditions. This often involves staying in tents and having little or no communication with the outside world, even if the training location is not that far away. What it boils down to for me—which is what matters, right?—is I don't get to see or talk to my husband for days on end. What it meant that day was I had no way to let Brett know about the news I had just received.

However, the Lord provided. Our sweet friends, Jared and

Britton, who were barely back from their honeymoon, came to watch Ransom on extremely short notice. They had only lived down the street from us for a few months, but they were very important months. Jared and Brett had been friends for a while, and Britton had married into the friendship. She ended up being among my lifesavers in coming weeks and months.

I love the way the Lord puts people into our lives at just the right time. Britton will always belong in my story, and for that I am grateful.

Leaving Ransom in capable hands, I headed off to the hospital by myself. Being without Brett was difficult in those moments. I was scared out of my mind, and wished I had him by my side. But God worked all things for my good, because instead, I learned to rely fully on Him. I had to do so. As I drove across Fort Benning—at the intersection of Fort Benning Road and Victory Drive, to be exact—I had a come-to-Jesus moment. In the midst of my tears, I confessed my powerlessness to help my babies. More importantly, I acknowledged God's *powerfulness*. I knew there was nothing I could do, there was nothing the doctors could do, there was nothing *anyone* could do for our girls, because they belonged to Jesus.

"You gave them to us," I sobbed out loud. "They are yours. Only you have the power over my babies' lives."

They were His. He knew it already, and I finally acknowledged it. Then, because I didn't know what else to say, I prayed a "please-please-please" prayer. This is the prayer one prays at rock bottom. When there are no words to express your desperation, all you can do is blubber out "please-please-please!" Truly, these are the best kind of prayers. At my lowest point, I realize God is the highest point. I see Him in His rightful place as Lord over all. When I'm not quite so desperate, I hold on to little bits and pieces for myself to worry about and try to fix. But that day, at the corner of Fort Benning Road and Victory Drive, I was desperate. The veil was ripped, and I saw just how tiny and fragile I really was. All I could say was "please."

I arrived at the hospital in Columbus, found a parking spot, and took the long walk to labor and delivery. I say long because it hurt to walk. Walking caused contractions, caused pressure, caused me to realize with every step how serious my situation was. It didn't help that when I arrived at labor and delivery, the nurses looked at me and thought I was there to deliver a full-term baby. This is not what a girl, barely 20 weeks pregnant, wants to hear.

I was in the hospital for about 18 hours, but it seemed like an eternity. The babies and I were both put on monitors to track their vital signs and my contractions. This first hospital experience was far worse than it needed to be because of some simple things that I, or a kind nurse, could have remedied. I didn't know I could ask to have the monitors turned down so I wouldn't have to hear them all night. I didn't know I could unhook the cord directly from my monitor, so instead I removed the sensors from my body every time I had to use the bathroom, repositioning them when I returned. I didn't know I could ask for the lights to be turned off when the night nurse left the room after her rounds. Small things, but along with the stress and worry I was feeling about our babies, they all added up to not much sleep. I was a rookie that night, but I would soon get a crash course in hospital care. If I had known more and was better rested, I would have handled the following day much better.

The next day, I met with the on-call fetal specialist, because Dr. Sheridan was out of town. I could easily brush over that little statement, "Dr. Sheridan was out of town," but I know it was not a coincidence. With all the knowledge we have gained now, we can clearly see Dr. Sheridan's pattern of inactivity. We did not know enough then to realize her lack of responsiveness to our twins' condition, but I count it a mercy she headed off to the Caribbean on vacation when she did. Because she was not there, I saw Dr. Milburn, the fetal specialist who was on call. He was a fatherly fellow, who was both kind and grim. He was grim because he recognized the dire nature of my condition.

Much later, Dr. Rivera, in Houston Texas, who would become one of our greatest medical allies in the fight to save our girls, told me when he first spoke to Dr. Milburn on the phone about my case, Dr. Milburn told him, "It is hopeless." Dr. Rivera, God bless him, said, "Send her to us. We deal in hopeless cases."

At the time, I didn't know any of that. I only knew my contractions were not getting any worse, so I would be able to travel to Houston for the surgery I hoped would save our girls. My overnight hospital ordeal had rattled my usual bright side view on things - enough to leave me with barely a shred of hope. This is what I wrote on my blog while I was in the hospital:

The doctor just left, promising an "early ultrasound" to check on the girls. I so, so dread this. Normally a mom delights in pictures of her children, but it is beyond painful to see them in their current states, with no power to help them. Ah, power. The power to comfort; the power to save. Such powers we as humans have been trying to master from the beginning. Yet with what success? This morning I read Isaiah 41, and its promises are what I must stand upon today:

The oppressed and the poor look for water but there is none; their tongues are parched from thirst. I, the Lord, will respond to their prayers, I, the Lord of Israel, will not abandon them.

I will make streams flow down from slopes and produce springs in the middle of the valleys. I will turn the desert into a pool of water and the arid land into springs.
I will make cedars, acacias, myrtles, and olive trees grow in the wilderness; I will make evergreens, firs, and cypresses grow together in the desert.

I will do this so people will observe and recognize, so they pay attention and understand that the Lord's power has accomplished this, and that the Holy One of Israel has brought it into being. Isaiah 41:17-20

Friends, I do not know what today brings, but I do hope you will see the ever-perfect Hand of God at work. I guarantee it will be perfect. Hard maybe. Seemingly tragic, or maybe hopeful and victorious, but whatever the case, may He be recognized as the author and accomplisher of this day.

When I read those verses now, all I can see is Tabitha. I see her little body, deprived of nutrients, and the Lord providing "pools of water in the desert" for her in some miraculous way we do not understand. Neither of our girls were abandoned. Both were cared for in ways only God could know and choose for them.

Chapter Six

With everything in place for my admission and surgery at the hospital in Houston, a few hurdles still remained. Brett was back home from the field, but before he could accompany me to Houston, he had to go back to work to get an emergency pass, permission from his chain of command to leave his duty station. Then, we had to get ourselves to Houston. Although our babies' lives were in danger, mine was not, so we were not eligible for medical evacuation. Travel costs would be up to us, so we bought plane tickets to fly out of Atlanta that afternoon. My parents would drive from their home in Nacogdoches, Texas, about two hours from Houston, to pick us up.

I drove myself home from the hospital to relieve my wonderful babysitters, Jim and Bonnie. Ransom was napping, so I thought I'd have a few minutes of peace to quickly pack our bags, but no such luck. Minutes after the sitters left, Ransom woke up screaming. I tried to comfort him and pack bags at the same time. Every few minutes I would have to stop and breathe because my contractions were coming on so strong. Somewhere in the mix, I looked up and saw a lot of time had passed. I realized if Brett didn't get home in the next five minutes, we would not have time to make the two-hour drive from Columbus to Atlanta in order to make our flight. If only he could get his leave forms filled out quickly. The five minutes came and went. Our chances of making the flight slipped away. There was no way we could get there in time.

I sat on the couch, sobbing. Ransom sobbing next to me. These are the moments when, as life crashes over me, and I come up gasping for air that I want to I cry out, "Why isn't God making this easier? It's hard enough as it is. Why add a screaming toddler, contractions, and a missed flight into the mix?" The answer is: I just don't know. I don't know except that all those things did force me to my metaphorical knees. I spent the next six hours in constant "help-me-help-me-help-me" prayers. These were much like the "please-please-please" prayers of the previous chapter.

Brett finally made it home and found Ransom and me, still sobbing. Brett piled all the bags into the car, and tried valiantly to lift me from despair. We headed for Atlanta, booking new flights on the way. We got there in the nick of time, and ran through the Atlanta airport, Brett, Ransom, me and my contractions. In Alanis Morissette "Ironic" fashion, when we got to our gate, we learned our plane was delayed by a lot. We sat with a tired two-year-old, me still having contractions, at an airport gate, for several more hours.

Finally, our plane was ready, and we boarded the flight from Atlanta to Houston. It was the longest flight ever in the history of the world. I don't remember how long it took to get there, so I'll just round it down to 5,798 hours. Sounds about right. These were some of the hardest hours, physically and mentally, of my life. By then I was officially ready for the Second Coming: "Come back already, Lord Jesus. Blow those mighty trumpets, because I'm ready to go home."

Airplane seats are not comfortable at the best of times. They are narrow. They recline about one inch. Perhaps this is stating the obvious, but they are not made for women in labor. Being in an airplane while having contractions was not only the worst thing ever, it was hell. My contractions were coming hard and fast and with every wave of pain, I would plead with God to help me and my two babies make it to the hospital in time. When I wasn't pleading with God, I kept telling myself it would end. That this flight, in all its painful glory, would one day be over. My body did not believe it.

When we reached Houston, my whole being was intent on making it to the hospital. Every ounce of adrenaline, every bit of energy, every fiber of my being was just focused on holding it together. By the time we got to baggage claim, tunnel vision was in full effect.

That's where I totally lost it. Contractions, fear, two tiny babies, missed flights, an unhappy two-year-old, and one extremely erratic courtesy cart driver left me heaving my guts out next to the escalator. The barfing was followed by uncontrollable sobbing and then breathing into a paper bag to prevent hyperventilation.

And that's how my parents found us at the airport. Yet in the midst of it all, God was caring for us in so many important ways we didn't realize until later. For example, we didn't know then that my obstetrician, Dr. Campbell, knew the general in command of the Fort Benning hospital. She called him late that night on our behalf to help with the approval process for my surgery. This connection sped up getting the clearance we needed. Something which would have taken days or weeks was taken care of in one day. Another blessing, the fetal specialist, Dr. Rivera, who would perform our much-needed surgery, studied and practiced medicine all over the world. He is from Spain, but he began working at Texas Children's Hospital in Houston the very month we would need his essential and specialized skills.

I am forever grateful to all the doctors who fought for our "hopeless" cause, but that realization and gratitude would come later. That Friday evening, all I could do was cry and try to survive.

My poor Papa navigated the medical district in the heart of Houston to locate the place that offered us a sliver of hope for our girls. Ransom was gleefully pointing out cars and trains from the backseat, oblivious to the navigation confusion and to his mother, who was again panting into a paper bag in the front seat. Finally, at well past midnight, for the three of us still on Eastern Standard Time, we found our way to the triage floor where I was checked in. Only minutes later, we met the surgeon, Dr. Rivera, who was soon to become one of my very favorite people. I would come to know his accent and his mannerisms and would learn how to interpret his bedside manner and tactics. At our first meeting, however, he sat calmly and reeled off the statistics and percentages for the various surgical options available to us. Trying to cut the tension with humor, I told him he sounded like a used car salesman. But in reality, we could tell it wouldn't take much selling for us to see what needed to be done.

In that conversation we realized everything about the girls' condition indicated that laser abrasion surgery was our best option. This procedure would divide the shared placenta in half, ideally giving each girl her very own lifeline. Also in this conversation, we realized for the first time it was our bouncing, rolling, flipping Priscilla, who was in the most in danger. The extra blood flow and fluids she was receiving were too much for her heart. Both girls had a scary road ahead.

By the time we left that meeting, it was somewhere around 2 a.m. on Saturday morning with surgery slated for 6 a.m. We went to my room in the triage unit to try to rest for the few remaining hours. We were scared, but we were also exhausted.

I was grateful for the exhaustion; otherwise, I don't think I would have slept a wink.

The previous days had been such a whirlwind. I had no time to second guess, to think twice, to wonder if what we were doing was right or wrong. We pushed forward with the knowledge that Bigger Hands were holding our lives together. Hands that, even in the smallest ways, were taking care of us.

In the months to come, I would spend more time in the triage unit and not all of it pleasant. However, the night before my surgery, when Brett and I were both tired and vulnerable, we were given an angel for a nurse. I don't remember her name, and I never saw her again in all my future visits to the unit. I wish I had. She was incredibly kind, taking care of details that allowed us the most privacy and best possible rest during those few hours before surgery. She even found crackers and cereal bars for Brett to eat since food service was shut down for the night. She asked Brett's name and remembered it. Most nurses we encountered on this journey, just called him Daddy, the usual title for husbands with their pregnant wives. Being called by name is a small thing, but it blessed us both that night. Finally we shut our eyes, and in what seemed like only a few minutes, I was being awakened to prepare for surgery.

Chapter Seven

General anesthesia could be harmful to the babies in their precarious condition. When I arrived in pre-op, the anesthesiologist, who would monitor me throughout the procedure, assured me she would keep me sufficiently sedated during surgery. The anesthesiologist's first name was Priscilla. Until that moment, although I loved the name, I had never met a real-life Priscilla. I took it as a little confirmation and reassurance from the Lord that this surgery was the right decision. Second-guessing and confusion would come later, but in the whirlwind of pre-op checks, lights, strange faces, and many fears, I was thankful to hold on to the hope her name offered.

Surgery went smoothly, with no hiccups or complications. My doctors were able to divide the cells of the placenta into two, giving each girl her own food source. The precision of this complete division was essential, not one shared cell could remain. If we lost one baby in the coming days, and any shared blood flow remained, it would mean death for the other baby as well. Also during the procedure, the doctors drained some of the excess fluid that had built up around Priscilla. She was still left with more than the normal amount, but to put it into perspective, after the surgery I was 9 pounds lighter.

Before the surgery, Dr. Rivera told us about the milestones that would mark our girls progression toward survival. Making it through surgery was first. The next 48 hours were crucial as they adjusted to the new conditions in utero. The next milestone would be if they could survive two weeks. After that, they were up against the high possibility of preterm labor, a different battle than the one we were currently fighting.

We were filled with such relief when the first ultrasound after surgery showed the beating hearts of both girls. We had cleared the first hurdle. We noticed Priscilla was moving much less than usual. Dr. Rivera reassured us everything could still be okay. In his kind way, he reminded us she'd had a pretty rough day and was resting. I took his words to heart and clutched the two pictures of Priscilla the doctors had snapped during the procedure. Not ultrasound pictures but real, live, actual pictures of her little face and one of her little feet. The angle during surgery didn't allow them to get any good pictures of Tabitha, but I know it was another sweet gift from the Lord to receive those pictures of Priscilla.

Dr. Benson, the chief of obstetrics and gynecology at Texas Children's Hospital, had been assisting in our surgery, and he and Dr. Rivera's kind words of encouragement echoed in our ears as we began our wait for the next milestone.

We spent the rest of the day in my hospital room wishing time would go faster. I remember being put on oxygen, "to help the babies," but don't remember being extremely worried. In fact, I don't remember much from the first day after surgery. I've asked Brett and my family to recount what they remember from that day, but even those stories do not jog my memory. I know I wrote a blog post asking for prayers for the girls and included a picture of my giant belly with a little heart shaped bandage over the new incision. The post was shared across social networks reaching friends, family, and many complete strangers, who then prayed for my girls and for our family. Our story was becoming more than just ours. It was becoming something bigger, and it was about to take its biggest turn yet.

The second ultrasound was on Sunday afternoon, well before the official 48-hour mark. Dr. Benson, after seeing the results from my first day's ultrasound, said he "couldn't stop thinking about it." So he came in on his day off to check. "Just to check," he said.

What a sweet mercy to have Dr. Benson come that day. With his expertise, perhaps he knew exactly what he was going to find. But instead of putting it off, or leaving it to another doctor, he followed up and followed through.

When Dr. Benson arrived, wheeling the ultrasound machine in front of him, Brett had just come back with Mexican food from Chipotle, my very favorite. My sister, Anna, my mom and I were sitting with me, and we were all about to eat our lunch. I remember how we all casually, yet curiously, leaned forward to see the ultrasound screen. And I remember the split second when we looked at Priscilla's still little body, and we turned to Dr. Benson for an explanation. Because there must be an explanation. Surely, she was just asleep.

"I'm so sorry," he said. Just like that.

Yes, the time between those two ultrasounds doesn't seem to exist in my mind. It's as if I went from one ultrasound—one with two hearts beating—to an ultrasound where only one heart was beating. There is nothing in between for me. I struggle to describe how I felt – the numb disbelief. In some ways it was similar to how I felt when I saw both girls on the ultrasound for the first time. Here I was, dreaming again, but now it was a horrible nightmare. Yet, even then, above everything else I was feeling, I felt the Lord's presence. It hurt so very badly to lose our little girl - to lose all the hope wrapped up in her little life. For a solid year, I could not eat Chipotle.

Everything seemed to hurt, but almost immediately, the words of an old hymn came to my mind:

When peace like a river attendeth my way,
When sorrows like sea billows roll;
Whatever my lot, Thou hast taught me to say
It is well, it is well, with my soul.

My mind was filled with grief, but I was still able to take hold of the last sentence. It is well.

The departures of the doctor and my family were a blur, and soon Brett and I were alone in the room. I remember wanting so badly to make him feel better, not in the selfless way it sounds, but more in a "so he can take care of me" sort of way. Rarely in our marriage have we both been equally low. One of the real mercies of hard times in marriages is *usually* one of us is able to be the strong one. In this case, neither of us could be strong. We had to turn to Him who knows all our sadness and grief. The only one left to lean on was Jesus. There in that hospital room, we prayed and wept together - pouring out our grief to the Lord and confessing He was still good. It was an important prayer to declare our Lord was *good* even though our baby girl was gone. It would be the legs on which we would stand from then on.

In our greatest time of need, when my heart was quite literally broken in two, I had grace upon grace. The Lord reassured me it was well, and I had to believe Him.

Now, I'm not a saint. I don't have special saintly powers that allow me to handle awful things better than other people. What I did have that day was supernatural strength. The Lord gives us exactly what we need in the moment we need it - dying grace on days we are dying. We certainly felt the sting of death that day.

It brings to mind when the children of Israel were hungry

during their time in the wilderness and God gave them just enough manna from heaven for each day. He told them very specifically not to gather more than they could eat in one day. The exception was the sixth day, when they were to gather for that day and the Sabbath too, so they could rest on the seventh day. Of course some of those rascally children of Israel—seriously, I'm *so* like them—didn't completely obey. They gathered a little extra when they weren't supposed to, just in case God forgot to send any the next day or something. It didn't do them any good, because the next day, the leftover manna was full of maggots.

I'm like that sometimes. I'm not quite sure God will provide what I need when I need it. I worry I'll be stricken, that I won't be able to handle whatever situation I'm in. When I start to worry about some unknown thing, I can't imagine how God will possibly be able to help me in that dreadful time of need. (Duh, because I'm not God.) Therefore, my worry turns into doubt, and doubt turns into fear. The book of Exodus gives the whole account about the manna. And the point of the story is God sent the manna for the Israelites for as long as they needed it, just enough for every day. Not more. Not less.

August 26, 2012, was the day we lost Priscilla. This was the day my heart was broken. That day, God gave me everything I needed to believe Him. Just enough.

The other remarkable remnant of grief was the gift of empathy I had never experienced before. As I sat in my hospital bed, beyond empty and grieving the little baby girl I never got to meet, a dear friend came into my mind. This friend had lost a twin when he was seven months old. It was like the Lord said to me, "Now, you know a tiny bit of her pain. *Now* you can really pray for her." So I cried for her too. Now I could truly understand the bottomless loss a child leaves behind.

I'm not one to compare painful situations. Comparison doesn't end well for anyone. And I also know losing my child doesn't mean I understand all grief. As awful as it was to lose Priscilla, I cannot imagine what it would be like to lose a child I'd touched and held and loved in person for seven months. Or 12 years. Or 25 years. Along with giving me just enough grace to endure my pain, the Lord gave me just enough empathy to feel at least a little of every mother's loss. It was a gift that hurt, but still a gift. This gift was one of many that Priscilla's life gave me.

Another was the gift to pray with my whole heart, with my whole soul, knowing what the Heavenly Father knows. He knows *exactly* what it's like to lose a child. He knows because He went through it. And the crazy part is, He did it knowingly. He actually chose to give up the Son He loved. For me. For you.

It was as if my Priscilla took me aside, just like the Priscilla in the Bible took Apollos aside, and explained more about the Good News. "Look here!" she said. "There is so much more to the story!"

The Lord miraculously got me through those first hours of loss with just enough grace. But in the same breath, I have to say, the next days were bad. I can't pinpoint when the days began to get better, but eventually some days did. Some days are still painful because grief never goes away.

It was such a comfort to us that Priscilla was named before we lost her. It reaffirms in my heart that she *was* ours, even just for a little bit, and we have every right to grieve her loss. And we still do.

The early days of grief were particularly bad, and I learned showers are the best place for serious crying. It saves tissues, because the snot gets washed away by the water, and the shower muffles my sobs so I can more freely let my emotions out.

One such shower sob-fest sticks out in my mind. I remember because, in the midst of the sobbing, I got pretty mad. I asked God why He would take my daughter away from me. It seemed so clear that Priscilla Beth had so much to live for and such a name to live up to. He answered by taking me back to the intersection of Fort Benning Road and Victory Drive, where I had admitted to God my daughters belonged to Him. At the time, I was praying more along the lines of "They're Yours, so You take care of them by getting them through this!"

But, when I remembered that prayer again, the stark, simple truth hit me. My daughters are His. Period. No strings, no conditions. He can do exactly what He chooses with them. I was beginning to see that Priscilla was loved in a way the rest of us could not imagine. My grief and sadness were still there, but even as I began to come to terms with our loss, the even more complicated truths about grief were becoming a little more clear. The major complication was that, mixed in with grief for Priscilla, was worry for my other daughter, for Tabitha. The best way to explain it is with ultrasounds.

My medical care in the following days included many ultrasounds and monitoring of Tabitha's heart. I lived for those reassurances Tabitha was still alive. Yet those same tests reminded me each time Priscilla was not. Over and over again in those following days, we'd have ultrasounds and I'd have to see Priscilla's little body not moving. Gone. Eventually, I had to make myself look away and ask the practitioners to tell me when her image was not on the screen. But when the girls were smaller and so close together, it was almost impossible to see one without the other. In an awful twist of fate, Tabitha was moving so much more than she had before, but right beside her was her sister, still and quiet. One bouncing girl, one still. On the one hand, it was like having to relive a bad dream again and again. On the other, I lived for those images of Tabitha. Each one gave me hope she was getting better - that she might just make it. Now all my hopes rested on her.

The first night after Priscilla's passing, as I got ready for bed, I was struck with an overwhelming sense of panic. I called the nurse and begged her to check for Tabitha's heartbeat. I couldn't sleep or calm down without having one last listen. Except when I was thinking about the loss of Priscilla, Tabitha's little life consumed my thoughts. My mind was constantly swinging from grief to hope. They were separate emotions, yet all mixed together. This was the beginning of our darkest "days between."

A few days later, I was released from the hospital with follow up appointments scheduled—still in Houston—for the end of the week. My doctors didn't want me to go to my parents' home in Nacogdoches, fearing I would be too far away from appropriate medical care in an emergency. It would cost a fortune to stay in a hotel near the hospital. We didn't know what to do, but an answer came quickly. A family friend with a home in the Houston area offered his house. He was working overseas and sent messages to us. "Please use my house," he said. "It's at your disposal. Stay as long as you need."

Again, our needs were met just in time, down to the last detail. We had a home for that week of waiting. It was a fully furnished house about 30 minutes from the hospital. It was pretty much the perfect set-up. Whenever I look back and I'm tempted to doubt whether God was there in our tragedy, I only have to remember the little details like this. God so handily put every need into place at exactly the right time. The outpouring of love we received each and every day, often from unexpected sources, was truly mind-blowing.

The house was in Humble, Texas so we dubbed our new home-away-from-home the Humble House. It was a perfect name because we were truly humbled by the kindness that allowed us to stay there. Prayers and messages of love and support from family, friends, and strangers were beautiful and continual.

They were my daily manna, feeding me hope when I couldn't feed myself. In my wilderness of fear, confusion and sadness, I took what God provided through the hands of others. I was learning that sometimes, when I'm at my lowest point, I must look to someone else to sustain me. Little did I know I would learn this lesson even better in the days to come. I would need every ounce of sustenance, every glimmer of borrowed hope.

Chapter Eight

One little detail that demonstrated God's perfect timing and provision happened when we first came to Houston for my surgery. Brett's brother and his family were in Texas on a missionary furlough and Ransom was able to stay with them while Brett and I were in the hospital. It was a gift; these family members we rarely saw, were not only nearby, but were also willing to take on toddler duty on short notice. I was glad Ransom was with people who loved him, but he and I had never been apart so long. It was heartbreaking for me to be away from Ransom, but it was reassuring to know he was spending quality time with his aunt, uncle, and cousins. When I see the pictures my sister-in-law thoughtfully took during that time, I am amazed by how much Ransom looks like a baby. He grew up so much during the following weeks and months.

One of the greatest parts of staying in the Humble House was having Ransom back with us. I needed to have my first baby back to soothe my broken heart. I needed to be able to hug my son as I mourned one daughter and feared for another. Also, having a toddler—who by definition, is fully wrapped up in himself—is pretty fantastic therapy. Cuddles, laughter, naps, dinner menus, discipline, schedules, toy options, all of it could fill the corners of my mind that felt so empty.

All the while, the Lord offered me wonderful friends, both old and new, to give comfort and strength. And He gave me His Scripture which spoke like it had never spoken to me before. But, I'm also not ashamed to admit that I watched really bad TV every single night. Bad TV—like all the seasons of *30 Rock* and the last three seasons of *Gossip Girl*.

Going to sleep and waking up are the absolute *worst* moments when dealing with the heavy blanket of grief and fear. Throughout the day, I could shrug off some of the weight. The duties and distractions of each day would pull at it and fray its edges. But, at bedtime, it became overwhelming, lying on top of me, making every breath difficult.

Yes, mindless TV lifted some of the grief and kept it at bay until whatever sleep aid I was taking could kick in. Televised comedy and fantasy were my drugs of choice. Personally, I think everyone needs some form of non-addictive drug to help them in these moments. Okay, somewhat addictive.

On the night before our follow-up doctors' appointments,

however, no amount of *Gossip Girl* could take away my mounting fears. Tabitha was still so tiny and the excess fluid that remained around Priscilla meant I couldn't feel Tabitha's movements to reassure me of her presence. When I was in the hospital, I could plead with a sympathetic nurse to put the heart monitor on one more time. Since moving to the Humble House, I had no such daily assurance.

Part of the follow up tests was the granddaddy of the heart monitors: an electrocardiogram, or EKG, of Tabitha. We also had an appointment with the fetal cardiologist. The night before I was scared of what all those devices might or might not find. What if she was quiet? What if she was perfectly still? What if she was gone too? God knows there's a time when neither TV nor sleep aids, Facebook messages nor anything else will bring relief. He sent us a perfect gift.

Brett and I were lying in bed praying for the coming day, for the appointments and the doctors and all the unknowns of our future, when I felt it: a perfect undeniable little flutter. Tabitha's first kick.

The Lord had answered my unspoken cries. He knew how much I craved reassurance as I went into the next day of doctors and machines. I needed a reminder of the One who was really in charge, the Author of life itself. No matter what my fears told me, or medicine told me, He was the one calling the shots.

I remember celebrating that first little kick when I was pregnant with Ransom. How wonderful and exciting it had been. Even if this second pregnancy had been run of the mill and perfectly average, we would have still celebrated the first kick milestone for all its magic. Under the circumstances, it wasn't magical; it was divine. Jesus was using this little life to remind me He was in charge. I went into my appointments the next day armed with the truth: Jesus is the author and perfecter of life, and He can be trusted with all our lives.

Tabitha's little flutter kick had repeated several times. I'm kind of like Gideon in the Bible who asked God for many signs. I needed multiple little kicks before I believed what God was saying. And He gave me what I needed. I felt confident we'd have a little alive baby girl the next morning at our check-up. Sure enough, we did, and everything seemed good-ish as we headed over to get my EKG and to see the fetal cardiologist. I say good-ish because seeing our two daughters side by side was still terribly hard.

The somber faces of the doctors didn't offer up tons of confidence. By the time I was lying on my back, watching the EKG technician run her wand over Tabitha's heart again and again, the little comfort we had gleaned from the first ultrasound of the day had slipped through our fingers.

Back and forth, over and over, stopping to listen, stopping to measure. Again and again. I'm sure they train these technicians in poker faces, but there was something about how much time she was spending hovering over Tabitha's little heart, measuring and re-measuring, listening and listening again. The way the light from her screen seemed to reflect in her watery eyes. *Were those tears?* I started to panic. My own very real tears started to well up and leak out the sides of my eyes, as we finally completed our EKG and were ushered into a little conference room.

We'd never been taken to a meeting room to discuss a medical test, so this was an alarming development. I was used to the whole sit-on-the-side-of-the-bed-uncomfortable-like-while-doctors -impart-information scenario, but this was all different. Also, we weren't just meeting with *any* doctor, we were meeting with Dr. Allison, the director of fetal cardiology at a world-renowned children's hospital. I guess that should have given me some warning even before we got there.

So, there we were, two very scared parents in a small space with a box of Kleenex and Dr. Allison, holding a piece of paper with a picture of a heart on it. She began showing us, Anatomy 101 style, just what those seeming *hours* in the EKG room had revealed.

Tabitha was not well.

The combination of 20 weeks of strain and constricted blood flow, plus the added strain of the surgery, had left her with an acquired heart defect. By the time the doctor was finished the heart diagram was a jumble of lines and squiggles and a hodgepodge of big words and various lists. It was a mess. The way that paper looked is a good depiction of how our minds felt. We had just lost one of our baby girls and we were shocked at the news we had a good chance of losing another. All the tears I'd kept in came pouring out. The calm composure that, for some reason, I felt was important to keep up around strangers, was gone. I sobbed there in that little conference room. I needed every last one of those Kleenexes as we listened to Dr. Allison explain Tabitha's condition. Her right ventricle was enlarged. The tricuspid valve was leaking. In its current state, her heart could develop pulmonary valve atresia where the valve fails to open, thus not allowing blood-flow to the lungs. Dr. Allison's words started to run together, and the pictures blurred on the page. But then my eyes came into focus on what Dr. Allison wrote at the bottom of one of the heart pictures:

1. "Newborn A-P shunt" (Blulock-Taussig Shunt) at birth
2. RPA- 3 to 9 months
3. Fontan Surgery- 2 to 4 years of age

Three different procedures. Tabitha could need three life threatening surgeries before she was four years old in order to have a chance at a normal life. Brett and I sat in complete and utter shock. Dr. Allison went on to say that there was a very slim possibility the heart issues could reverse themselves.

"I've seen it happen, but not often," she said. "In a month we'll take a look to see if there is any change at all. At that point, we'll be able to tell if she might be able to recover from this." Then Dr. Allison gave us names of three different doctors in Atlanta whom she had personally trained in the surgeries Tabitha would need if the healing did not come. These were doctors she felt sure would do a great job.

In the midst of my tears, Dr. Rivera, who had joined us for the last part of the consultation, said we were also welcome to come back to Texas for any of our care. He probably says that to all his patients who come in for surgery. How could he know I'm the kind of girl who clings to those kinds of invitations? Still, that day it was all just words. Words, words, words. They all ran together, and the only thing I could feel was numb shock.

I know I was in shock because Brett and I talked very little about what we had heard in that room. Over a year later, I brought it up on the phone with my mother-in-law, and she said we had never fully explained to her what was said that day. Was it because the issues were so complex? Or was it because we just couldn't fully handle the truth: the truth that the battle for Tabitha's life was not over. She survived the two-week post-surgery marker we'd been praying for, but she was definitely worse for wear, hanging on by a thread with a severely damaged heart.

I left the appointment feeling completely beat up. I had used up all my own personal faith that things would turn out, and they had not turned out. Not according to my plan. I knew God was good, and I believed with all my heart He was in control, but I no longer had any sense of security that He would save Tabitha. I was a theological mess.

I was left with an overwhelming desire to go home. I simply wanted to return to a semblance of a normal life. I wanted tangible, manageable problems I could fix. And I had a ton of those. We were headed home to real life. My doctor had put me on bed rest with bathroom privileges. No lifting, no making dinner, no driving. I could go nowhere except to doctors' appointments twice a week. This, with a husband who worked upwards of 65 hours on a *good* week and a toddler who needed constant care, including lifting, snuggling, diaper changing, and food-making. Yes, I had a ton of immediate problems to keep my mind busy.

We flew back to Atlanta and made the two-hour drive home. With the help of a good friend, we immediately put together a toddler bed for Ransom that very evening. There was no way I could lift him in and out of the crib, so this seemed like a good first problem to fix. Now I could technically be left alone with him while Brett was at work. One problem down. But the other problems flooded around me. I felt like I was drowning in problems.

As it turned out, I was my own biggest problem. I began to realize it was hard to accept help even when I really needed it. Real talk moment: I'm a fixer. I'm a doer. I like to do. If I start to feel a little lost, a little out of control, I do something so I can feel better. It's funny, right? It's funny God would force me, the ever-constant doer, to not *do* anything.

My favorite coping mechanism was yanked away from me. My mind went back to that very first little lesson, 18 weeks earlier, when I read the poem about Sabbath waiting. All my previous waiting seemed like the minor leagues. We had just entered the majors, and boy, were times tough. Those first few days back in Georgia seemed harder than even the plane trip to Houston; yet there was no particular new awfulness. Sometimes it's harder to have faith on the normal days. Not in a hospital; no family around. No hope of an ultrasound in a few hours or a doctor standing there to answer questions. Above all, I was feeling a letdown after the abundance of grace that poured out during the stressful days in Texas.

So what about the other days? Normal days when all I had to do was take care of Ransom? Except, I really couldn't do that. I was forced to simply be still, and wonder about tomorrow. That's where it got to be difficult and the little lies crept in. I started to wonder if any of our big prayers would be answered - conveniently forgetting the ones already answered. I wondered if Tabitha would be taken from us too. I wondered if we'd find the help we so desperately needed to take care of our house and home when I could do nothing - again forgetting how God had carried us so far. I forgot it all, and I felt so empty.

Is there grace on those ordinary days? Yes, there is. The Lord can speak even in such moments. One day my Bible reading was Luke 5:5, where Jesus is in a boat with his soon-to-be disciples, and he tells them to let down their nets. Peter replies,

> *"Master, we have toiled all night and took nothing, but at your word we will let down our nets." (ESV)*

This verse struck me hard. I had become that kind of fishermen, toiling in my own strength, getting nothing in my nets but an old Coke can and some rusty nails. When the Lord asked me to lower my nets again—to have hope again, to trust Him again—would I do it? This passage says nothing about whether Peter believed this time would be different. Later, when they do pull in a huge load of fish, he falls down at Jesus' feet and asks for mercy. So maybe Peter didn't really think things would change. Even if he didn't, he was still obedient.

That is where my own grace-filled truth lay during those days of doubt. My truth lay in being obedient – in lowering my nets into seemingly empty waters and trusting the Lord's purpose for my nets to be there. What would I haul in? Only the Lord knew, but whatever it would be, it would be about Him and not me. It would teach and mold and change me, but first I had to be willing to lower my nets again. I had to trust the Lord to do great things.

This became my daily choice when, only a week before, we had been hurt so very badly. I needed to let down my nets, to trust in our Lord to care for us and provide for us. Yes, we trusted Him; we knew He was good, and yet life had left us as empty as the disciples' fishing nets. Here He was showing us that if we just let down our nets for *Him*, He would most definitely fill them. So that is what we did. Each morning we would wake up empty and put down our nets. Invariably, He would fill them up each and every day. To continue with the analogy, what we caught in our nets was truly a surprise.

Chapter Nine

When I say we had an empty net each morning, I mean Brett and I woke up almost every day knowing that alone we could not even do the smallest practical tasks of the day. My being on bed rest meant I could do very little. Brett's work schedule kept him from being able to take over duties at home. The duties like taking care of a toddler all day. It was during this period when we were introduced to a thing I call The Art of Being Served.

The hardest thing for a doer like me is letting someone else be the doer for me. It is torture. In Christian circles, particularly among Christian women, many of us have forgotten about an essential part of our walk with Jesus. He exhibited this at the end of His time on this earth when He washed the feet of the disciples. When Jesus came to the feet of Peter—a guy I totally identify with—Peter says, "Oh no Jesus! You're not going to wash *my* feet! That would be so embarrassing!" and Jesus is like, "No. You've got to let me do this, or you won't be able to be a part of what I'm doing."

Peter's response is common among all of us Christian women doers. We are not about to let Jesus wash our feet. It would be so embarrassing. He's our Leader, our Lord, our King. It would be awful to let Him serve us. He'd see we haven't had a pedicure in months, that we've got bunions, and maybe an ingrown toenail. Horrors!

Okay, so that's a bit silly, but here's the not-so-silly truth. What about the toilet? Seriously. What if a friend offered to come over and clean your toilet? Maybe some people are like, "Cool. That'd be awesome. When can I schedule you in?" But serious doers? No way. If someone were coming to clean a toilet for us, we'd have to clean the toilet before they got here to clean it. I'm not even kidding.

I used to freak out when we were having people over for dinner. The house had to be in perfect condition. I'd spend the last hour before they came cleaning out from under our bed, just in case someone tripped next to our bed, fell on the floor, and glanced under there. How awful would it be if they saw a dust bunny? I know how ridiculous this was, and it got in the way of my entertaining schedule. I'm much less likely to have people over for dinner if I feel compelled to deep clean the refrigerator before they come. Having my first child pretty much cured me of compulsive under-the-bed cleaning. My house cleaning standards dropped to just above hazard mask required. However, there was still some curing that needed to be done in my heart. I needed not only to allow people to see the dust bunnies under my bed, I had to allow someone to clean them up.

So began my first lesson in The Art of Being Served.

This lesson was very hard because it meant giving up almost everything I took pride in - all the abilities in which I invested my misplaced self-worth. I had to hand them over to other people and allow them to do everything for me. To say it was humbling is putting it mildly. During this season, I must have written, "I am so humbled by your love…" about fifty million times in thank you cards. I was being humbled right and left. I was humbled because it turns out I had been getting misplaced satisfaction from all my doing and not enough from my Lord and Savior.

The humbling started bright and early on the first day back in Georgia when Brett left for work, and my friend Melissa came and took over the household duties of the Wilson home. She became our family sitter.

Melissa and I became friends when our husbands met at an army school and Brett invited them to our Bible Study. I was giant-pregnant with Ransom, and soon after we met, Melissa became tiny-pregnant with Emmy. Our babies were born seven months apart. We became fast friends, taking our kids to story time at the library; sitting in one another's toy-strewn living rooms, laughing and crying over the life of a military wife and mommy.

I've always admired Melissa's incredible ability to be crafty. I mean, Pinterest crafty, not Harry Potter crafty (though I'm guessing she'd be a Hufflepuff if sorted.) The girl is constantly making something beautiful out of nothing and looking good while doing it. She is also eternally sunny and laid back, something I'm continually pretending to be but can never *quite* pull off. She never fails to amaze me.

Oh, did I mention her husband was deployed when she became our family sitter? She was currently performing the roles of Mommy *and* Daddy at her house while her husband was overseas fighting for freedom. I had great plans to relieve some of the pressure for her in the months ahead, but great plans are destined to change. Instead, Melissa found herself taking on several more roles at my house during the next few weeks. It's a funny thing. I thought I knew Melissa really well. We'd had plenty of serious conversations about family, life, goals, and dreams. But it wasn't until she was folding my underwear and putting it in my underwear drawer that I realized I hadn't seen anything yet! I was about to learn about another side of Melissa: she is an organizational wizard. I had failed to appreciate this talent because, let's be real here, I was probably too busy pushing myself into the role.

The second day Melissa showed up at my house, she was armed and fully prepared to take charge. She gave me homework:

writing out medical release forms for anyone who had to watch Ransom if I was away and writing up information sheets of important numbers and contacts in case of emergency. These practical things had completely left my mind due to, well, all the other stuff consuming my mind at that time. Melissa brought in the practical element I so desperately needed but was too scattered to take on myself. She also made rules for other people who would come to help me. She put a sheet of paper on my refrigerator that read:

> "Abigail is under NO CIRCUMSTANCES allowed to lift anything or bend over and pick anything up. She is not allowed to walk around the house for any length of time and can only be sitting up for a few minutes at a time."

I, of course, said this was ridiculous, but laid-back, calm and sunny Melissa got all hardcore and did not back down one inch. She went so far as to not even trust me with the refrigerator rules. She would call the other ladies who had volunteered to family-sit and go over the rules with them before they came to my house. My friend Tina caught me trying to unload the dryer, and I tried to convince her it was cool. Tina informed me Melissa had warned her this might happen.

"She told me not to back down," Tina said.

Oh.

I smile even now, because Melissa was doing pretty much exactly what I would do under the circumstances. She did it with much more grace than I would have, I might add. Even while I was fighting her efforts, she knew I needed someone to crack down on me, to tell me to go lie down, and to give me simple, tangible, practical tasks to keep my mind busy. Anyone who knows me knows calendars are my love language. I'm a planner and a list maker, and I love a good schedule. Up to that point, I didn't know Melissa had this scheduling superpower. Even if I didn't want to admit it, I needed her to take on roles she had never taken in our friendship, and she was ready. Melissa set up Google Calendars, so our friends could easily see what our needs were and how to meet them. They could sign the online calendar to bring meals, take on housework, toddler duty, whatever they could do.

We all have our pet ability - that one thing we know we're really good at. When the right circumstances arise, we're ready to rush into battle, yelling "I've got this!" over our shoulder, proudly brandishing the sword of our special skill.

Part of my Art of Being Served education was learning how to let someone else brandish her sword. I was touched beyond belief when my friend Melissa rearranged her busy life to show up almost every day to lay the smack down on the unorganized pitifulness of the Wilson household.

Long distance friends pretty much rocked my world with their ability to come up with the most creative and supportive ways to love our family. Several friends pooled their resources to buy us a deep freezer - what a thoughtful and generous gift. They figured rightly, that we'd receive many freezer meals to help us with food prep during the season ahead, so we'd need a place to put said food. Another friend, who lived thousands of miles away, sent us gift cards to a company that delivers frozen meals.

Even with so many generous and creative friends, I fought the urge every night to worry whether the next day's needs would be met. Seems I would have learned by now to trust the Lord to provide. He didn't just provide for our physical needs; He also sent remarkable love and encouragement through the hands of many people. I received cards and packages that lifted my spirits, and boy did they need lifting.

The generous hearts of these people changed me forever. I used to think that if my condolence cards were not the most meaningful in the world, I shouldn't send it at all. The perfectionist in me focused on myself and not the recipient. If I couldn't do it perfectly, I wouldn't reach out

I discovered that reaching out to someone in need is far more important than flowery words. It was the love in those gifts that was important. Every expression of care and concern was perfect because of the love they conveyed. These generous givers took the step; they put our family's need above their own limitations. Never again will I make excuses that keep me from reaching out to someone in need or in pain.

Melissa and her cadre of volunteers took care of us for two weeks. It seemed even longer to me. At the time, of course, we didn't know how long we would need this level of care or how long we would have to depend on our friends' kindness and willingness to serve. I wondered each day when they would be exhausted by our need. I was certainly exhausted by it. The Lord cared for us so faithfully through the hands and hearts of our friends, but I still managed to worry daily about just how and when He was going to "fill our empty nets."

At the three-week point, our need coincided with my friend Tabitha's yearly visit. Tabitha is the dear and steadfast friend for whom our Tabitha was named. She lovingly makes time each year to visit us from her current home in Canada. Even though we usually choose a random month and a week for her visit, it always ends up being perfect timing. That's how God works and also how our friendship seems to flow.

This particular visit, however, could have seemed like the worst possible time ever, at least for Tabitha. What is usually vacation time for her was replaced by a week of stepping in to run the Wilson household. Tabitha proved herself more than worthy of her biblical namesake by doing our laundry, caring for Ransom, preparing meals, and cleaning my refrigerator. A true friend is someone who will check the expiration date on your Italian dressing and chuck it in the trash. (Six months past due, baby!)

Tabitha also learned how impossible it is to fold laundry with a two-year-old in the room. I've got pictures to prove she did the same basket twice before finally giving up and accepting how much a two-year-old loves a good clean pile of laundry to nest in. Sounds like the worst vacation ever, in my humble opinion. But what a gift she was to us. I was so blessed to have a whole week of Tabitha.

Having Tabitha to care for our family also provided the mental space Brett and I needed to start thinking past tomorrow or the next day. Depending on our friends was becoming more difficult. People had their own families to care for and lives to live. We couldn't go on like this indefinitely. Hiring someone to do everything we needed was financially impossible.

Still, we had to take my health into account. Every doctor's visit showed more strain and more progression toward early labor. The amount of time I would be able to stay out of the hospital seemed to be about as short as my cervix (miniscule). Oh, yes, I'm always one for a good short cervix joke, but the danger to baby Tabitha if I went into early labor was no laughing matter.

Of course our Tabitha was our greatest concern. The chances of her heart not needing intervention were apparently slim. We were ticking off the days of what we called the magical month deadline Dr. Allison, the fetal cardiologist in Houston, had given us for Tabitha's heart recovering. It seemed like such an arbitrary amount of time to determine something as momentous as the healing of our baby's heart. At our weekly ultrasound appointments, the doctors in Georgia still saw a very sick heart. In fact, they were already talking about sending me to Atlanta for delivery, which meant I'd have strangers deliver our daughter. Not what I wanted for her or for me.

Brett and I lay in bed one night discussing the pros and cons of me going back to Texas for the remainder of my pregnancy. I very much did not want to go. It meant being away from Brett.

It meant leaving the comforts of home, relying on a whole new set of friends and family for care and support. To be honest, it meant going back to a place that held the hardest memories of losing Priscilla.

Then it hit me. None of that mattered. The first person I needed to consider was our baby Tabitha. She was the one most in need of my care. Perhaps it was easier to think about Brett, or Ransom, or even myself, but Tabitha's life and health had to be our primary concern. At the end of every day, I wanted to be able to say to her, "I did everything in my power to protect and keep you safe." If not, I wasn't doing my job as her mommy. And that job, Tabitha's mommy, was vital. Others could help me care for Brett, Ransom, even myself. As long as I carried Tabitha in my womb, I had to be the one to provide the care she needed.

As I've already said, those two weeks in Georgia of being waited on hand and foot were painful. This was primarily because I had to hand over the responsibilities that gave me self-worth and satisfaction. Awesome mom? Nope. Other people were taking care of my two-year-old. Awesome housewife? Nope. Other people were doing a better job than I could manage. (See expired Italian dressing.)

Whatever the demands of motherhood, whether it's the routine of thankless daily tasks, or the humility of handing those tasks over to someone else, it is always one hundred and fifty thousand percent worth it, even when it's time to make difficult choices.

We finally made ours. We decided the best way to care for all of us, especially Tabitha, was for me to take Ransom and stay in Houston as long as necessary to protect this pregnancy and give Tabitha a fighting chance.

First, we had to get there, which was easier said than done. Our first trip to Houston had been in emergency mode. If that method has one silver lining, it is the lack of time to consider all the complications. We just did it. This time around, I had the luxury of a few days to realize how many roadblocks we faced to get back to Texas. The biggest being, this time I would have to go without Brett because he had to be at work.

As I tell this story, I realize some people may wonder why Brett wasn't able to get more time away from his army duties during these crucial and difficult times. I can only say that everything we were going through with this pregnancy was uncharted territory for us. So when Brett's commanders were unwilling to give him time off and were unsympathetic to our family situation, we assumed that was the way army life had to be. Our experiences since then have given us more perspective, and now we too realize the inflexibility of the leadership under which he served at the time. Could we have demanded more support and understanding? Maybe, but at the time we didn't know how.

Although the army—at least in the form of Brett's chain of command—was not supportive, many other people stepped up to help us in any way they could. My Aunt Donnave is a prime example. She has dropped everything for my family and me countless times. Need someone to drive cross-country to help transport household goods? Done. Need someone to take care of a first-time mommy whose husband is away for military training? She's there. These are just the more recent drop everything moments she's given to us. She's given so many I've lost count over the years.

Aunt Donnave calls this her "gift of availability." I think it's so inspiring. It sounds simple in words, but in deed, it means she puts the needs of others ahead of her own plans and priorities. This is an incredible and beautiful thing. I used to think I might be able to practice the gift of availability someday, maybe when my children are all grown and I am retired. Spoiler alert: I was about to learn that people from all seasons of life can give this gift. When someone is sick and needs a meal, or a drive to the doctor's office, or when a friend's car breaks down and she needs a roadside rescue, or a last-minute drive to the airport, being willing and able to provide is really important. I learned just how important from the people who were willing to share their gift of availability with me.

Aunt Donnave came to my rescue. She dropped everything and came to Georgia to travel with Ransom and me to Texas. Of course, it wasn't that easy. Things just wouldn't go according to plan. We drove to the airport only to find our flight had been cancelled. Bad weather or something like that. We would have to come back the next day, so we drove all the way back home again. At home that night, instead of celebrating that Brett and I had another night together, I threw a royal fit about how things were so hard and nothing was easy. *Why couldn't things go the way I wanted them?*

Back at the airport the next day, Ransom also threw a royal fit. Imagine a cute, slightly sticky, very tired two-year-old standing in the middle of the pedestrian thoroughfare between airport gates, his face to the heavens, mouth open, screaming because he wants to *push* the stroller not be *in* the stroller. Now imagine this toddler confronted by a mammoth, sweaty pregnant woman with a crazy look in her eye. It wasn't pretty. Why no one called child services is beyond me. I am grateful no one did. *I mean, come on Ransom! Can't you give me a little bit of a break? Must you want everything your way? And must you always try to do things that are too dangerous or just plain too grown-up for you?*

After we recovered from the stroller incident and boarded the plane, we encountered another tragic misunderstanding. After a cool visit to the cockpit, Ransom thought he was going to get to drive the plane. This is a common misconception, to be sure. It's totally reasonable for a two-year-old to think he's able to pilot an airplane. But the octave Ransom's scream reached when his misconception met cold hard reality; well, that was something truly remarkable. It's now humorous to think of a two-year-old who thinks he's qualified to fly a large jet. Or his casual assumption that no one would think twice about his little arms pushing a stroller around a busy international airport. Oh yes, two-year-olds. We expect it of them and they all grow out of it, right?

When we finally arrived in Texas, my mom met Aunt Donnave and Ransom and me at the airport and took us back to stay at the Humble House. It was late and I started casually giving my mom and my aunt their instructions for the evening.

"You can get Ransom ready for bed, and then I'm going to come upstairs to read to him and put him to bed." I said very matter-of-factly. " Ransom has his bedtime routine, and he's used to me reading him his bedtime stories and putting him to bed. This is a new environment and I want to have things as normal for him as possible."

I laid out my case, and it was a good one. However, my mommy was there. And she put her foot down.

"No, you can*not* climb the stairs to Ransom's room."

Cannot? Now it was my turn to throw a fit - again. I let my poor mom have all the worst of me, venting my frustration about all the things I could not do and all the events that refused to go my way. Afterward, my mother gave me a firm talking to, reminding me of Tabitha and how I had to put her health first. She pointed out that I couldn't just do what I wanted. I had to do what was best for Tabitha. Probably, if I'd been two, she'd have given me a good spanking. Instead, she put my son to bed while I cried about it in my room.

This 28-year-old—going on two—could most definitely climb stairs and fly planes. Of course, if I had been flying the plane I would have run squarely into the giant roadblock the following week would bring.

Chapter Ten

We traveled to Houston over the weekend, so bright and early Monday morning I had my first doctor's appointment to get settled into the new location. The doctor took one look at me and pretty much freaked out. I didn't blame him. I was freaking out on the inside pretty much all the time. The doctor, who incidentally I never saw again after that day, was not impressed by the condition of my rapidly thinning cervix. Convinced that labor was imminent, he would not allow me to leave. Instead, he sent me straight to the main floor of the hospital for observation. I must have looked too calm because he told me that, aside from Tabitha's heart problems and lack of lung development if she was indeed born in the next few days, she could also have certain neurological issues that could take months to a year after her birth to manifest. He said Tabitha could have many delays in her physical and mental development that he could not even begin to predict.

"We need you to be prepared for these risks and possible outcomes," said Dr. Whom-I-Would-Never-See-Again.

He followed up his diatribe by presenting me with various options to stave off labor and help Tabitha's body survive in the event of birth, which in his medical opinion, would be in the next few days.

All I could think was, Whoa! I just got here. My son and I are both coming off of some major fits. We're not even settled in yet. Ending up back in the hospital was not what I had on the agenda for my first week back in Texas.

My agenda notwithstanding, I was soon alone in a hospital room after getting the first round of steroid shots that would give Tabitha's lungs a boost. (It's a giant needle that they stick in a particularly vital place for those who enjoy sitting and other lounging activities. It ain't no joke.) I'd had to explain to my two year old he was going to have to leave Mommy here at the hospital and go back to the Humble House with Spicy, which is what he calls my mom. It was a heartbreaking thing at the time even though Spicy was thoroughly up to the task. I contacted Brett, states away, to talk about Tabitha's current situation and try to relay all of the information to him about what was happening and the decisions we would have to make. Oh, and I hadn't eaten anything since breakfast. I guess I was due for a breakdown. So I sat in a hospital room and cried and cried for what seemed like the millionth time. Tear fests were fast becoming the go-to event in my life, and I was dominating at them.

I stayed in the hospital a few days until my doctors felt like we were out of danger for the moment and then went back to Humble with strict instructions to not do anything. When I got back to the Humble House with Ransom, I proceeded to do all sorts of things not defined under the "don't do anything" category. Even then I did not fully understand the importance of staying off my feet. So day after day it was a fight to get me to stay on the couch.

As for Brett and me it was just a fight period. Being apart was necessary at the time, but it came at many costs. Distance was definitely not helping either of us in the empathy department of marriage. For a whole week, people from my hometown were taking turns driving the two hours to watch Ransom and police my activities. My mom, my sister, and my mom's best friend, Billie, who is like a second mom to me, all took their turns watching Ransom under my increasingly impatient, worried, and watchful eye. In spite of being ordered to do almost nothing, I wanted to do everything. I was wracked with guilt over not being able to care for him myself. It didn't help that Ransom had chosen this time to fine-tune his fit-throwing skills. Events were ripe for disaster.

Brett came into town for a weekend visit and to leave us with a car for our time in Texas, and we started things off with a good old-fashioned couple's spat the first morning. Never mind that he had worked a week of 12 hour shifts and left at 4 a.m. to drive 13 hours to Texas. I was annoyed he didn't seem to "get" the situation, and he was confused by how my words clearly didn't line up with my actions. I'd been taking my Sunday best face off with Brett a lot over those last few weeks. He'd been witness to some of my quality fits, and I was just getting started. Our relationship would definitely falter and sputter during the coming months. In stressful times it's interesting how we put the most pressure on those we know love us and will continue to love us even when we're acting just like the two-year-old who lives down the hall.

I'm not airing our dirty laundry here just for kicks. I'm being honest because I think our situation is probably not unique. It's difficult to deal with a serious family issue and not create rifts in the relationships with those we love most. I wanted Brett to be my strong rock of a husband, when he was not only fighting the same battle I was, but some extra ones as well. The distance, the stark difference in our everyday lives, plus the drastic differences in our personalities dialed up the pressure. Life was hard. We had a lot going on. We may have thought our relationship could take a backseat during those days of grief and struggle, but we could not afford to allow that to happen.

We managed to have a good weekend with Ransom who enjoyed having one parent who could hold him and run after him. On Sunday afternoon, the mild cramping I'd been experiencing started to get a little more intense. And then a lot more intense. Around the time Brett should have been heading back to Georgia, he was instead driving a crying Abigail to the hospital.

The good thing about our drive to the hospital that Sunday afternoon was that it was football season in Texas. Everyone was home watching the game, and traffic was nonexistent - a rarity in Houston. As we sped down an empty six-lane highway, once again traveling with contractions, I fell back on my "please-please-please" prayers.

"Please-please-please, don't let this baby come!" I cried, over and over again. All the awful things the doctor had told me the week before were circling my brain. I knew Tabitha was better off staying in the womb as long as possible. Why couldn't I put that into action? Why couldn't I stay on bed rest the way I needed to? Bed rest needed to be not only staying in bed doing nothing while resting my body - which I wasn't doing very well. It also needed to be staying in bed doing nothing while resting my worried mind. In other words, the most impossible situation for me. I was on a roller coaster that wouldn't stop. No matter how hard I tried in my own strength, I wasn't making the cut. So my body stepped in and revolted, sending me back to the hospital.

The procedure for admission in the triage wing is fairly standard. Gown. Vitals. The usual questions. The nurse's aide who met me at the triage wing that day was incredibly perky. She was incredibly nice. She was also incredibly slow.

"Let me hand you a gown to put on in the bathroom," she

chirped. "Oops! Forgot a clean gown! Let me go get one. Oh! I see the bed doesn't have a pillow! I'll grab one while I'm grabbing the gown!" She returns with gown in hand, "Oopsies! I forgot the pillow! Ha, Ha! Silly me!" She leaves to get the pillow without handing me the gown.

This sitcom sketch seemed to go on for hours, but finally I was in a bed with the now familiar monitors hooked up to my stomach. My annoyance level was at a nine. My stress level was at a ten plus, and my patience level was at negative one hundred. Miss Perky nurse's aide was the final straw. A strained marriage, a struggling two-year-old, a pregnancy rife with trouble: it all swirled around me.

Dr. Rivera, who performed the surgery to divide the placenta, came to see me and brought reinforcements, another specialist, Dr. Sing. When they stood at the end of my bed to discuss my situation, it was painfully obvious what my diagnosis was: I was a bed-rest failure. Dr. Rivera and Dr. Sing stepped in to save me from myself. These doctors are not typical obstetricians, but fetal interventionists. Their bread and butter is performing remarkable surgeries on babies in the womb and doing research to develop ways to treat sick babies in the future. In other words, super-hero doctoring - the stuff that makes modern medicine miracles happen. Watching over a bed-rest failure is well below their pay grade.

But Dr. Rivera generously took me on as a full-time patient in his very first month officially on staff with the hospital. As a package deal, I also got Dr. Sing. The day I met him, he had just begun a prestigious fellowship in fetal intervention which was the first of its kind. These were my doctors: a world renowned expert in fetal intervention and a fellow in fetal intervention who'd won a place to study with some of the best doctors in the world.

And while we're at it, this was my hospital: one of the few facilities in the world to offer such an extensive range of fetal and maternal care. The building was so new the new-car smell wasn't even out of the halls, and doctors and nurses were still finding their way around. This environment—an incredible new women's medicine wing, an already amazing children's hospital, and two doctors who arrived to work there in the month we would need them—was not all about me. However, I'm in awe when I recognize our situation, which the Lord knew about from the very beginning, happened *exactly* when this amazing facility and talented practitioners came together.

Dr. Rivera and Dr. Sing stood at the end of my bed and told me I needed to stay in the hospital and, that I would probably have to stay there a long time.

"We're just trying to get you to 28 weeks," they said. I was at week 25. It was September, a little over a month since our surgery, and each day seemed to be an uphill battle. The thought of making it to 28 weeks seemed impossible. Looking down the barrel of spending the next three weeks in the hospital drained the faith right out of me. To make matters worse, Brett had to go back to work. He had to leave Houston only hours after getting the news I would be staying there indefinitely.

My sister, Anna, had been watching Ransom at the Humble House. When she was relieved by the next saint on the toddler-watch list, Anna came, three-month-old baby in tow, straight to the hospital to spend the night with me so I would not be alone. Yeah, that's right. Whenever they do that reality game show where people compete as to who has the best sister, I'm going to throw down, "stayed in my hospital room, sleeping on a teeny-tiny fold out chair with teeny-tiny baby next to her." And the show will be shut down. I will win all the prizes. Everyone else will just go home shaking their heads wondering how I could have been so lucky. I win.

Not sure my sister is so lucky because what followed will go down in history as one of the worst nights ever. I wasn't kidding when I said this hospital was all shiny and new and state-of-the-art. I had been here twice before, and both times I was amazed by the amenities in each room: flat screen TVs, beautiful couches that convert to beds for guests, floor-to-ceiling windows, and granite counter tops. By far the most impressive were the bathrooms. No joke, they were nicer than any bathroom in any house I've ever lived in, and significantly nicer than a lot of hotels I've stayed in. And I like really nice hotels. If I'm going to sleep somewhere other than my own bed, then it might as well be better than my own bed. Mottos to live by, people. I blame my parents. On my sixteenth birthday, my parents took two of my friends and me to the Four Seasons Hotel for one night. My three friends and I piled into one bed, which you'd think would be uncomfortable, but you would be wrong. Despite having arguably too many people in one bed, it was still like sleeping on little clouds. I announced at breakfast the next morning that I could live in hotels the rest of my life. What I really meant is I could live in *luxury* hotels. Since then, I've been a bit of a pill about hotels I will or will not stay in. I'm not proud of it. I'm just pointing out what spoiled-rotten looks like: It looks like me. So believe me when I say those hospital bathrooms were incredible, the showers had water jets. Water jets. I rest my case.

Now for the punch line: The triage room where my sister stayed with me had no shower. Sure, it had a "toilet room," but no shower, bathtub, or any place to wash except in the sink. I guess they had to cut corners somewhere to save up for the fancy bathrooms elsewhere. I was there for two days, using the communal showers, which were down the hall, around a corner and to the left. Uncool.

It was not a great start for what I was told would be a three-week hospital stay. My husband was in another state. My son was in another town. Sister and baby sleeping on a rickety chair: there was so much to cry about, so we did. After we'd had a good cry, my sister and I put on our big girl panties and started trying to make the best of a bad situation. We scavenged around the room and found one of those acrylic bassinets used for newborn babies in the hospital. We figured Anna's 3 month old could sleep comfortably in that. It was better than joining Anna on the rickety chair, and she figured using the bassinet would be easier than going all the way back to the car to get the pack-n-play. This was definitely the case since she didn't have a stroller with her since she had not counted on an overnight hospital stay as part of her trip.

Anna and I both needed showers, so we sucked it up and took turns going down the hall, around the corner, and to the left to take our showers. I spent *my* time in the shower crying because, as I mentioned before, it's a great place to cry. Besides, I kind of hoped the nurses at the nurses' station would hear me and feel sorry for making Mrs. Supposed-To-Be-On-Bed-Rest go down the hall, around the corner, and to the left just to take a shower. They didn't, of course.

When Anna went to take her shower, she didn't think it was a good idea to leave the baby with me. I suppose it was the whole "not supposed to lift a thing" mandate, or maybe it was the breakdown I'd had earlier. She opted instead to put her little one in the bassinet, which was on wheels, and push her down the hall around the corner and to the left to the shower. And I think this would have gone well, but unfortunately she had to pass the nurses' station, and the head nurse caught sight of the three-month-old in the bassinet. Apparently this was against the rules, so adding insult to injury, the nurse confiscated the contraband bassinet. Anna was forced to go all the way to the parking garage, carrying the baby, to then bring back the pack-n-play (and baby of course) over a sky bridge, up an elevator, and then down several long halls back to the room. And just to be *extra cool,* the nursing staff watched my sister juggle all of this without offering to help.

So we had yet another cry. To this day I still do not know how my sister did it. I spent the next two days using the shower down the hall, and my sister had to go out to the nurse's station to try and track someone down to help us anytime I needed anything. I guess triage wasn't used to having long-term guests. When I mentioned to my doctors in passing that I didn't have a shower, since it seemed counter-productive to my bed-rest rules to do so much walking to take a shower, my doctors looked in my bathroom to make sure I hadn't missed the shower. When they didn't find one either, they moved me to an official room. I went through two double doors, a little way down another hallway where I was met with lovely rooms and a wonderful and attentive staff. It was like night and day. And I happily got reacquainted with the glorious shower with jets and the gorgeous tile. I hoped that here I could finally rest and focus on what I really needed to be doing in that hospital: beginning to heal.

Chapter Eleven

The events of the previous weeks had me tied up in knots. Slowly but surely, as I woke up each morning in the hospital, receiving good care from kind staff, my mind, body, and spirit began to accept the rest they needed. The Lord had been trying to speak to me all along, but I had not been very receptive. But He'd used those around me to speak to me, because my own mind was so muddled. A person who will speak truth during those muddled times is a treasure. Hold on to those people. Finally, I was beginning to hear again the truth God was speaking to me, and the very first thing He spoke to me was about my children.

The very first verse God had given me at the beginning of my pregnancy, Isaiah 49:23, came back to me now.

"Kings will be your children's guardians, their princesses will nurse your children …"

When He first spoke this verse to me, it was vaguely encouraging. Now it was a scarily accurate account of what was happening. Priscilla was in the arms of the King at that very moment. With me in the hospital, and Brett tethered to work, Ransom was in the hands of "princesses," all those wonderful family and friends who had taken on childcare for an extended period.

Ransom was one of the main reasons I was in the hospital. For the life of me, I couldn't stop parenting him when I was with him. Bed rest was nearly impossible for me when he was around. I was incapable of letting go. The weekend I went into the hospital, Megan, a family friend, had offered to come and take care of Ransom at the Humble House. Part of me wanted to bemoan the timing - of all the weeks for my little boy to be with a non-family member. Until then, my mom, my sister Anna, and our close friend Billie, who was like family, had been caring for Ransom and me. Now, when I wasn't able to be there, Ransom's well-being would be entrusted to people he didn't know. I thought it would be terrible. But it was perfect.

Megan had volunteered to join Team Abigail/Ransom Watch, but now that I was in the hospital, she would be caring for Ransom. Megan and her family attended my home church when I was growing up. Since then she had moved to Arkansas, and I was living in Georgia. Though we were far apart, Megan and I had this in common: no matter how far we moved, no matter how many new and wonderful people we added into our expanding spiritual family, the church in our hometown would always be home. In that way, we were still family, and Megan volunteered. A home school mom, she packed up her youngest two boys and headed to Texas.

Who is better than family to watch over a two-year-old little boy? Answer: a mama who's raised six kids of her own, and two young boys who are experts at playing with blocks and cars and trucks, and who bring cool toys along with them that are downright irresistible to a toddler boy named Ransom. Ransom's response to all this: "Mama who?" Megan was truly a godsend, and she came at just the right moment. She helped relieve my worries and helped me loosen my grasp on Ransom just a tiny bit more. She cared for Ransom and brought him to see me each day so I could sit in bed and watch him play hide-and-seek in the hospital wardrobe. When he was not with me, Megan sent me pictures of Ransom playing with her boys. Her pictures reassured me he was happy, carefree, and perfectly fine.

This was the balm to my soul and the push I needed to make my last big leap. It was time to send Ransom to stay with my parents. I had to allow others to "nurse my children." With me in the hospital, it didn't make sense for someone to come all the way to stay in the Humble House to care for him. We would send Ransom to my parents' house where they could take on the task of his primary care with the help of the many other family members and friends in our hometown. My Papa, who had long ago won awards amongst my friends for making the best packed lunches in the world, returned to making a little person's lunches. This time preparing beautifully presented bite sized meals for an unappreciative 2-year-old. In fact, as a prominent member of his community, my dad and Ransom became a common sight around town. Papa pulling a red wagon with a happy little boy in it to his various civic engagements. The thought of my son spending quality time with my dad made me happy, but unfortunately, it would mean I would no longer get to see Ransom's little face every day. My parents would bring him to see me as often as they could, but a daily four-hour round trip was impractical. I knew it was for the best, and I knew it was the right thing to do, but it still broke my heart.

Letting go of my little boy needed to be a step-by-step process for me. First, I had to get used to having others take care of him while I was around. Then, having others take care of him while I wasn't around but could still have one visit from him every day. Finally, I had to turn him over to our family for days and days at a time. Yes, little boys need their mommies, but mommies also need their little boys.

At the time, the Lord reminded me of the story of Hannah recorded in the first few chapters of I Samuel. Without realizing it, He had been teaching me about Hannah from my first prayer at the corner of Fort Benning Road and Victory Drive, when I had confessed the truth that my girls were not my own. They weren't. Ransom wasn't either. He belongs to God as much as Priscilla and Tabitha. The fact that he was outside my body and in good health didn't change those facts in the least. The Lord chose me to be their mother. What a gift indeed, but ultimately, they are still His children. My time with them is His gift to me.

Now as I read Hannah's story in the Bible again, I noticed for the first time how Hannah said she would bring her son, Samuel, to the temple when he was weaned. He was probably three years old. Yeah, I may have known that little detail from Sunday school or something, but it didn't hit me until I had my own son to compare with it. Let's just say my mind can barely fathom the lesson - for all our children. My children, whom I want to hold so tight until they start to wiggle and pull away. The children whose well-being occupied my thoughts from the time I first knew of their existence. These children do not belong to me. The sooner I acknowledged it the way Hannah did, the better. The sooner I knew in my heart of hearts that the Father of my children, of Ransom, Tabitha and Priscilla, is the one in control, not me. Incidentally, He is my Father too. It didn't make it much easier to let Ransom out of my sight, but I did understand that there had never been a time when he was only mine. I had to remember the truth: Ransom was just on loan to Brett and me.

Even with that very spiritual view, being apart from my son was one of my biggest struggles over the next few months. When he came to visit, he would come into my room, give me a hug, and then climb up onto the couch where he could look out of the floor-to-ceiling windows. There was so much to see: planes flying by, skyscrapers being built near the hospital, and teeny tiny ambulances driving down below. It was really a two-year-old boy's dream in some ways, and I thank God he was so easy to please in so many respects. But those hospital visits were hard for everyone. Saying good-bye to him at the end of a visit was awful. Seeing that little two-year-old with his wild and crazy hair (he always looked like he needed a haircut), face always just mildly sticky, pulling his little robot-shaped backpack on wheels away from my bedside broke my heart in pieces. Spending five hours in the car with a two year old every weekend so he could see his Mommy for a few hours was not easy on anyone involved, yet our sweet family managed it almost every single weekend. In fact, when I think of my own Mama faithfully teaching school every day and then returning home to a rascally two-year-old waiting by the door for her to give him undivided attention, it only seems fair that she would get her weekends off to recover and get much needed rest. But instead, she spent most of those weekends faithfully driving him to visit me, without complaint. I think there were maybe three weekends all told where I didn't get to see Ransom.

And then there was technology. Glory, glory, Facetime! How thankful I was for those Facetime calls. Half the time they would have to be abruptly ended because somebody needed a spanking or a timeout, but I felt better just getting to see Ransom. The little dude miraculously was born with the gift of gab and really did have the vocabulary and enunciation of a child much older. I suppose God knew it would be needed for all that long distance communication with his parents. Ransom had a funny way of making conversation if he couldn't think of anything off the top of his head. Sometimes he would resort to talking like an eighty-year-old grandmother: "And how are you today?" or "It's a beautiful day in the neighborhood, today!"

Ransom learned quickly how to navigate between the different authority and parent figures in his life. For instance, Brett's mother, his Nana, allowed him to have his dear, beloved pacifier anytime he wanted. Mommy and Daddy only allowed him to have it during sleep times. Ransom loved this extra perk about being with Nana. When his Nana brought him to visit me at the hospital, and he trotted confidently down the hall to my room, knowing exactly where to go after many visits, he stopped in front of the door, and turned and handed his precious paci to Nana before entering my room. He knew Mommy would most certainly see it and take it away. This boy had things all figured out. I had my worries about my baby adjusting to all the changes in his life, but he took it all in his two-year-old stride.

The first week I was in the hospital was also the time for Tabitha's next EKG - the magical month had come to an end. Dr. Allison had ordered a follow up six weeks after the last one when she warned us about the possibility of heart surgeries in our baby girl's future. We had prayed. Many had prayed. Really, praying was all we could do. There was no remedy except to keep Tabitha in utero as long as possible and pray for miracles. As I prayed for a miracle for Tabitha, I heard the Lord speaking. When I first settled into this new hospital life, accepting the need for rest, reading the Bible wasn't a struggle. When God spoke, however, He didn't say what I expected. In fact, as soon as He spoke the words into my heart, I knew I'd better write them down. We were taking sharp turns down uncharted roads almost every day and I knew our story could change in a moment. I needed to keep up with what the Lord was telling me, so I wrote what He said:

All the worry seemed to come to a head for me today in a powerful way. Amongst the lots o' tears:

It's a new morning, and tomorrow is the all-important cardiology echo where we will find out if our prayers have been answered in regards to Tabitha's heart. We will find out how difficult the coming road may or may not be. And there is something I need to say before we even find out where our future lies. I need to say it now because it's important that the result has no weight upon this truth.

The fifth chapter of Luke tells the story of Jesus healing a paralyzed man who was desperate to be healed. His friends made a hole in the ceiling of the crowded room where Jesus was teaching, and lowered him down so Jesus would see him. And see him, He did. Jesus said to the paralyzed man, "Your sins are forgiven."

Yup. Sins. Sins can often seem pretty intangible. In fact, depending on our sin, we can even get pretty good at covering them up. For many of us, we can sadly learn to live with our sins on a day-to-day basis. But not being able to walk? Not being able to walk is hard to cover up, hard to ignor.

So, of course, everyone there who witnessed Jesus' words started grumbling. For one thing, who does He think he is? Healing sins! That's a big claim, and one not so easily proven. So, Jesus, knowing their hearts, said something else, "Which is easier? To say, 'Your sins are forgiven,' or to say, 'Arise and walk?' But, so that you know that the Son of Man has the authority to forgive sins, Arise and Walk."

I was struck over the head by this because it was so very clear what was more important to Jesus. It was not whether or not this man spent the rest of his earthly days on a cot. After all, those days are relatively short. Jesus cared so much more about the man's heart. The heart is eternal. The heart is what affects every other thing we do and experience. Above all, it affects our relationship with our Father. To be able to have a relationship with the Father is to experience the greatest Peace, the greatest Love, and the greatest Acceptance one could ever know. These are the things that Forgiveness brings.

I felt the Lord reminding me so strongly that through this whole experience with Priscilla and Tabitha, we have prayed for healing after healing. And often we have gotten very caught up in the present needs. Wouldn't it be great to walk on our own again? Wouldn't it be great not to have to rely on someone else for literally everything? My life has a lot in common with the paralytic right now. Wouldn't it be wonderful if Tabitha was born healthy? All these things remain our most fervent prayers, but I know that whatever has happened and whatever will happen is important. It will draw us closer to our Lord Jesus. It will somehow help to refine and strengthen the bond of love and peace and acceptance we so desperately need from our Father in heaven. As for my daughters, they are already His. If He decides to heal Tabitha, as He did the paralytic, it will be a glorious day. But even if healing doesn't come tomorrow, it will come, and the more important work is already being done in our hearts.

Those words were some of the truest words I've ever been

given. They summed up our entire experience. The Lord will do just about anything on this Earth to have a relationship with His people. He loves us. He loves His children so much He will allow them to go through hell if that will draw them into His arms. Isn't that strange? I know I don't usually look at my challenges that way. Yet, the more I tell our story, the story of Priscilla and Tabitha, the more I realize how the Lord slowly heals the wounds in my heart, allowing me to walk without pain. There have been times, even in writing this story, when I doubted I'd ever get up and walk. But, with time, I believe I am walking again, and I believe, just like the paralyzed man, I am not only walking, but I am changed on the inside. God is healing my heart of the effects of sin. That is the real miracle.

On the day of the EKG, my ever faithful Mama took off work and drove to Houston to be with me. Of course, Brett was at work in Georgia and if my mom hadn't been there, I would have been all alone. I didn't know what kind of news I would receive, and I couldn't imagine not having someone by my side. Sure enough, the EKG process was almost as painfully long as the first one. Once again, I searched the eyes of the technician in vain to glean any information. Finally, it was time to meet with Dr. Allison, and the news was hopeful. Tabitha's condition was better. Not good, but better than before. The doctor impressed upon me again that Tabitha needed to stay in utero as long as possible. This we knew. Essentially, those last six weeks had been good. Things were looking better, but they were not perfect. There was a lot of damage in Tabitha's little heart, and the best treatment would be keeping her heart inside of me long enough for it to heal. The miracle Tabitha needed had a name: Time.

If, on that day, the doctor had told us Tabitha's heart was completely healed, we would have been shocked. We would have been excited! We would have told everyone we knew. But, as time went on, the initial miraculous aspect would have faded into the everyday. That's the funny thing about life: the miraculous gets normal pretty quickly. Fortunately, God knows this about us, so sometimes He gives us a miracle in small doses, and allows us to keep praying for the next one. The fact that Tabitha's heart was healing was a wonderful answer to prayer. Now He gave us a new, seemingly impossible, miracle to pray for: A full-term baby.

Chapter Twelve

A few days later, our prayer for a full-term baby saw its first big test. My friend Esther took time off from her job—unpaid vacation time—to come and sit with me for a week. I have rockin' friends. I really do. Esther had been staying with me a few days, long enough to get into a nice little routine of waking up, running to Starbucks down the street for Pumpkin Spice lattes, while I wrote my morning blog post and checked in on Facebook. Then, it was on to morning rounds and answering my doctors' usual questions: "Any contractions? Any pain? Changes in bowel movements? Blurred vision? Is the baby moving?" Next, was the morning baby check where the nurse would hook me up to the monitors for an hour to record Tabitha's heart rate and her movements. Esther and I would have lunch, read or watch something on Hulu until time for dinner. Afterward came nighttime rounds and another baby check, followed by my nighttime meds, which included the lovely sleeping pill that allowed me to rest. Now that I was settled into a routine and was more relaxed, I was taking only half a dose. I'd take a shower and then drift off to lovely blissful sleep. It was a routine, and I've already said how much I love a good routine. In fact, things were working out so well, I was starting to get comfortable. The trauma of the last few weeks of constant unknowns and continual changes were starting to seep away.

And then one night things were different. During the evening baby check, Tabitha's heart kept slowing way down and taking a little bit too long to speed back up again. The nurses were concerned and told me they were going to leave the monitors on for at least a portion of the night. I figured this would be annoying. Tabitha now liked to move around and move away from the monitors. Many times in a one-hour check, the nurses would have to reposition the monitor to find the heart rate again. *What a drag! I won't get any sleep.* So that night I took a whole sleeping pill and fell asleep to the sound of the heart monitor beeping.

I woke up the next morning to the sun shining brightly. I looked over at Esther who seemed to be waking up a bit slower than normal. It seemed like any other day, but while Esther was gone on our coffee run, I started to have weird snippet flashbacks of doctors standing at the foot of my bed, monitors beeping, statements like, "We'll have to take her to the OR if …" I could hardly wait for Esther to get back so I could ask her what had happened.

During my time in the hospital, as I think of all the wonderful women who sacrificed their time and resources to come and stay with me, I know there were no coincidences. Each one of those women came at the right time, for the right purpose. I smile now, knowing how perfect it was that Esther was there for this whole experience that I can't remember. I can't write about it effectively, but Esther was a creative writing major. She actually has a degree qualifying her to do what I needed, to write about that night for me. Here are her words:

> I woke up somewhere around 2:30 or 3 in the morning hearing a new beeping sound I hadn't heard before. I lay there for a minute to be sure the beeping was in our room and not the nurses' station, right across the hall. I was on the verge of getting up and checking with the nurses to make sure everything was as it should be, when one walked in casually, and adjusted the monitor, turning up the volume only slightly, so I could still barely hear it. I sat up groggily (it takes me a while to become fully awake) and asked her if everything was alright. She said yes, everything was fine. Abigail didn't move a muscle.

> I turned over to face the windows and tried to go back to sleep, but I knew that beep had been a different one than any I'd heard before. When you're in a hospital day in and day out, you hear a lot of beeping and a lot of buzzing. But after you've been in the hospital for a few days, you pretty much know what all those sounds mean. I couldn't be sure it was the heart monitor that had beeped in Abigail's room, but something had beeped whereas nothing had beeped the three previous days, and that fact kept me from falling back

to sleep for a little while. I must have barely dozed off when an alarm went off in the nurses' station. I threw my covers off and sat straight up on the couch where I had been sleeping. This was definitely not a normal beep or buzz. It was very similar to the one you might hear on someone's iPhone. You know, the immediate-attention-necessary "maaaah maaaah maaaah" one? Yeah, that sound was going on in the nurses' station outside the open door of Abigail's room.

In about the amount of time it took me to fully process the situation, three nurses were in the room, taking stations around Abigail's bed. She still didn't move, and, for one tiny moment, I wondered if the alarm might be for Abigail herself. But then I remembered the sleeping pill. The nurses started taking her vital signs and repositioning the monitor, and Abigail began to stir. As soon as I heard the nurse who was adjusting the monitor whisper to another "It's too slow," I stood up and walked to the foot of Abigail's bed. The three nurses were at the head of the bed, so I couldn't get to her hand, but I figured holding her ankle was second best. I figured she would need consistent human contact with the nurses buzzing about efficiently. I'm not really sure whether it was more for her or me.

Nurses came in and out of the room, each of them adjusting the position of the monitor, none of them satisfied with what they found. In the midst of all the organized chaos, Abigail remained still, maybe sighing or stirring a tiny bit (by this point, she was so used to nurses coming in and out at all hours.) I went back and forth between trying to comfort Abigail (which wasn't really that necessary) and trying to decipher the graphs printing out of the turned-down heart monitor (I wasn't very successful) and praying for peace for both of us.

Finally, one of the nurses came into the room and turned up the monitor just enough that I could pick up on the sound. I knew they were right. The heartbeat was much too slow. About the time I heard the slow heartbeat, the monitor went silent. Maybe the nurse had been adjusting and moved it too far, or maybe Tabitha had moved out of range, but she couldn't find it again. "I've lost it," she said to another nurse.

Then the resident came in. It's taken me longer to write this, but it was only about three minutes from the time the alarm went off to the time he arrived and took control of the situation. As soon as he walked in, he began speaking in a calm, cool voice, giving instructions to the nurses. Abigail woke up then. Even in her sleepy state, she knew something was up if a doctor was in her room in the middle of the night. She sat up and asked, "What's wrong?" The resident assured her he had no concerns, that they were just having a little trouble finding Tabitha's heartbeat. "Okay" said Abigail, and laid her head back down. This time she remained awake watching the doctor as he took over adjusting the monitor. Soon, another doctor came in. Now there were eight people in the little hospital room—four nurses, two doctors, Abigail, and me—all of us listening for anything resembling a heartbeat. Beeps, buzzes, and alarms notwithstanding, the room felt absolutely silent

Then we heard it. Quiet at first, then strong and steady at Tabitha's normal speed as the resident found exactly what he was looking for. All eight of us let out deep breaths we hadn't known we were holding. The nurses walked out to the nurses' station, and the doctors stayed inside for just a moment to make sure Abigail was settled. "Keep her awake" they told me since they wanted to come back in and talk about what had happened after they discussed it briefly with the nurses. Abigail and I talked quietly (mostly me talking, and Abigail "mmhmm" ing), and the doctors returned shortly.

The resident stood quietly beside the head doctor while he explained to us what they thought had happened. During the night, Tabitha had gravitated toward the sound of Abigail's heart for comfort and had moved so far towards it, that the monitor had begun to pick up the much slower beat of Abigail's heart instead of Tabitha's. This set off an alarm because the rate was much too slow for a fetal heartbeat. The resident had realized the monitor was positioned very high, so moved it back down to find Tabitha. At the end of the doctor's explanation, he asked Abigail if she understood, and she nodded her head. "So Tabitha is okay?" she asked. The doctor said Tabitha was fine and had never been in any danger.

"Okay," Abigail said, then turned to me, and said, "You need to remember all of this so you can tell me in the morning. I won't remember." Then she laid her head down and went back to sleep. The doctors moved between her room and the nurses' station for another 20 minutes or so, checking on Tabitha, reading the graphs, and discussing things under their breath, but they seemed relaxed and unconcerned, so I lay back down and tried to sleep.

I must have fallen asleep, because I woke the next morning to sun streaming in the window, and Abigail calmly reading blogs on her iPad. After I got dressed, Abigail asked, as usual, if I would mind heading down to Starbucks to pick us up some coffee. I usually enjoyed the little walk in the fresh air, but today my mind was preoccupied. I wondered, the entire way there, whether I should bring up the night before or let Abigail do so. I wasn't even sure she remembered any of it. When I got to Starbucks, Abigail's doctor was walking out the door with his coffee "Well," he said, raising his cup, "we both need this today, huh?" I grinned and agreed.

When I returned to Abigail's room, I handed her the coffee and settled into my sunny corner of the couch. "Hey Esther?" she said, "Something happened last night, didn't it?" I smiled, and told her the story...

So yes, Tabitha was fine, but I still read Esther's words with a chill in my heart. What happened could have been something entirely different, but I'm grateful for what I learned from that experience: it's best not to get *too* comfortable. From then on, I refused my sleeping pill, no matter how uncomfortable my night was going to be. I didn't want to be half-drugged while making important decisions about my daughter's future.

But, let me take a step back for a minute and talk about how totally awesome Esther was in that situation. It was a lesson I learned repeatedly: as independent as I wanted to be, I very much needed friends. I needed the wonderful people the Lord graciously provided at every step. As I continued my education in the art of being served, I learned how much the little things can mean on the receiving end.

Esther was just the first of several incredible women who sacrificed their time, leaving jobs, homes, and families to come and care for me over the next few weeks. My sister had sent out a distress call, and it was humbling to see these ladies set aside their own lives for a while to come and sit with me.

When Esther showed up, the doctors and nurses kept asking if she was my sister. In some ways we could be sisters. Both our families grew up in the same church, and I remember when Esther was born. I went with my mom to drop off a meal for her parents as they settled into having a baby. She was the first of three gorgeous daughters. I would watch and her and her younger sister, Sarah in the nursery while our parents were in Wednesday night prayer meeting. Later, after her baby sister, Abigail, was born, I became their official babysitter. Mostly, though, we played hard together. Many years later, when I was a new college graduate, she and some other high school girls would come to my house every week for Bible study. I watched them as they graduated from high school and made their first steps into the grown up world. By the time Esther came to be my hospital sitter, we were bona fide friends. As she sat with me there in the hospital, she told me about her experience working full-time at a Christian camp and what the Lord was teaching her.

Obviously the exciting night adventure Esther wrote about was probably the most memorable (or unmemorable, in my case) part of her stay. All of my time with her was precious. The conversations that filled our time together remain fresh and meaningful to me.

Jennifer was the next to come. I had known her all my whole life, yet I didn't feel like I knew her at all. Again, she was from the church in my hometown. She is older than I, but younger than my parents, so we hadn't spent a lot of time together. In fact, I don't think we'd ever really talked for longer than a few minutes. When I saw her name on the sign-up calendar I could hardly believe she was willing to come sit with me for so long.

Then she arrived, deposited her bags in the corner, ignored the couch and plopped right down on the bed in front of me. Then we talked in earnest, and I learned quickly that Jennifer likes to be in physical contact with the person to whom she is talking. Her intensity carries right on over into the depth of her conversation. Rarely in life are we gifted with uninterrupted time and space for conversation, but I had such a gift with this amazing lady. I picked her brain about raising boys—she has three—their family's decision to send their kids to a private school until high school, and her oldest son's misadventures and the unique mission field where the Lord called him to serve.

She told me what it was like being adopted and some of her experiences volunteering in social work. She told me what she gleaned from the last sermon at church and what the Lord was laying on her heart for the future. It was a relatively calm point in my hospital stay, and Jennifer's personality was perfectly suited to use this quiet interval wisely. She helped me get to know the caregivers I saw every day. She leaned in and asked personal questions. Through Jennifer I learned where my doctors were from, how many children the nurses had, and why the nurse's aide wanted to be a caregiver. It was almost embarrassing how little I had learned about these people I saw every day. Jennifer changed all that. She helped me by asking the questions I was embarrassed to ask, but needed to know, regarding my care and Tabitha's condition.

Allowing Jennifer to ask questions I was too overwhelmed to ask was incredibly helpful while she was there and in the time ahead when I would need all the information she gleaned. I have a feeling she would be surprised to know how much the conversations we had that week helped to inform areas of my life I didn't even know would become important to me later on: adoption, raising sons, children in crisis. Jennifer knew the often-overlooked art of asking meaningful questions.

Each of the women who took time out of their own lives to sit with me would probably be surprised by how significant their presence and their actions were to me. I've mentioned it to a few of them, and they've all shrugged it off. Maybe they only see what they did at face value for the practical help they offered. They gave me much more than that. Even more than their time, I learned so much from their willingness to step in and watch over me. They were each at different seasons of life: married, single, retired. They had varying occupations: a teacher, a full-time graduate student, a stay at home mom. They all had different worries in their own lives, different priorities, and one could argue, they all had plenty of excuses for why they didn't have time for Abigail Duty. Thankfully they did not use any of those excuses. In those days between, as I was forced into stillness and waiting, I did not have to sit alone. I had wonderful women ministering to me the whole time.

Having someone spend quality time with me has always been at the top of my list of ways I receive love, and each of those lovely ladies had a unique opportunity to fill me up and teach me through their actions. As my time in the hospital plugged along, however, I learned first-hand there were countless ways for someone in my circumstance to be loved.

I've never felt like I've been a very thoughtful person. Maybe because I'm not very empathetic. I definitely have never been very imaginative when it comes to helping those in the hospital or those who are sick. My "let's fix this" mentality gets stumped when I can't simply make them better. If the doctor is in charge of that, what is left for someone like me to do? God knew my lack of imagination and decided the best way for me to learn how to give empathetically was to experience it on the receiving end from my beautiful community of loved ones.

Flowers, for instance. It seems cliché, but flowers really do help turn a hospital room into a much more appealing place. A person in the hospital has the unfortunate fate of having the exact same view every single moment of every single day. Brightening up that view with something cheerful and colorful was exactly what my wonderful friends did for me.

My devoted people didn't stop with the typical hospital tokens, though. One friend sent cute little fall decorations to put on my window sill. As a bonus, those little pumpkins traveled home with me. They grace our Thanksgiving table to this day, reminding me how much I have to be thankful for. The same friend also sent hand soap for my bathroom and a hand towel to go along with it - all pumpkin-themed. Since I looked more and more like a pumpkin every day, it was probably the most appropriate theme she could have picked. These simple additions made my hospital bathroom less sterile, more homey. I remembered my friends' sweet love and support every time I washed my hands, which was a lot. A pregnant woman on intravenous fluids has many opportunities to visit the restroom all day and all night.

I received so many wonderful care packages while I was in the hospital. Mail day was by far one of the best parts of my week. One friend sent handmade toys for Ransom to play with when he came to visit. People sent magazines and books, and when I finished with them, I sent them out to the nurses' station where they had a second and third life. I learned it doesn't take an expensive gift to make a person in the hospital happy. The diversion of receiving and opening a new package was a gift all on its own.

I learned a lot about gift giving and receiving while in the hospital. When you're in the hospital, opening a package may be the only fun thing on the agenda for the whole day. Even the simplest gift would make my day. I delighted in every package of Post-it notes and every shade of nail polish I received. A package of gum was wonderful for its ability to distract me for a few precious minutes. It was also useful when my doctor came around at the crack of dawn when my teeth and mouth were not at their freshest. Lip balm was also useful for the dry hospital environment.

Considering how many thank you notes I needed to send out, pens and note cards were much appreciated. One friend who works in the post office sent me a variety of stamps. Not just the "Forever" flag stamps, no way! She sent Looney Tunes and flower stamps, which were not only cute, but very helpful for mailing thank you notes. Little things really do make a difference.

Some friends sent me cute loungewear. After wearing the same five sets of clothes for over a month, it was a treat to have something new to put on. It was as though my dear friends stepped inside my mind and sent me what I needed before I even realized I wanted them. Though it wasn't what was in the package that mattered most, it was the hands and heart behind the package that perfectly delivered the love I so desperately needed during those days in the hospital.

One day, a friend who lived in the Houston area brought me dinner. She packed up a simple home cooked meal. Now that was nice enough, but she stepped it up a notch and served it on real dishes. She spread a cloth napkin on my lap and presented me with a lovely plate and matching utensils. I felt like I was home. I felt normal. Having real dishes was the most incredible touch. For the first time in months, I did not feel like a patient. I felt like myself. It was the most healing bowl of chili I've ever had.

The lesson to me became clear as it was repeated over and over again through the generosity of friends who gave in innumerable ways. When you allow yourself to be used, you make yourself available for the supernatural work of God to work through you. Each package I received was exactly right for the moment I received it, fulfilling either practical needs or the needs of my heart. Each note of encouragement spoke perfectly into my hidden heart, the part that was especially tender on that particular day. These moments were not accidents. They were not just reminders of my friends' and family's love. They were also reminders of my Lord's love. Then I should not have been surprised that each of my friendly sitters also came at exactly the right time. Perhaps this was most obvious to me when Amy came to visit.

Chapter Thirteen

Amy and I have been friends since the second grade, making her, by all accounts, more a sister than a friend. The fact that she has stuck with me for two decades testifies to Amy's loyalty. She and I had bonded over our love of make-believe: mostly Barbies and adventures in the woods near our homes. We made it through the bumpy middle school years through sheer will and a lot of hormonal tears. And we had remained friends in high school, where our dark senses of humor had gotten us—okay, mostly me—in trouble. During our college years, we took different paths, me to New Zealand for college, her to a Christian school in Oklahoma. My faith grew stronger in those years, and our lives and choices began to look more and more different. When I headed back to the States after college, married Brett and became a bona fide housewife, Amy was working toward her master's degree and then her doctorate.

Our lives looked as different as one could possibly imagine, yet, on a weekend in October, she dropped all her career-building plans and came to take over bedside duty. She came for a weekend that turned out to be one of my most eventful times in the hospital. Honestly, who better to be there than the friend who saw me through my ugliest haircut in third grade, stood by me through puberty (not pretty for anyone), who had visited every place I'd ever lived, including New Zealand, and who had witnessed all my major life events to that point. I don't know how many people get to have second-grade friendships that last a lifetime, but, Lord knows, such a gift can't just be put up on a shelf to be admired every once in a awhile. Nope. That friendship is a gift to use. And boy, did God put Amy to use that weekend.

The floor was weirdly empty that Saturday night, so when my nurse had trouble finding Tabitha's heartbeat, she called in another nurse on the floor to help. I wasn't too concerned. Since the surgery, Tabitha moved a lot. Surely this was just run-of-the-mill stuff. I'd spent all day on the monitor that day, and the noise and nuisance had faded into normalcy. I had grown accustomed to Tabitha being difficult for her daily tests. I'd spent part of the day in hog heaven, despite all of the monitors, because Saturday was Ransom day. His visits were much too short, but I lived through the rest of the week on the strength of those visits with my rascally little boy.

In a military marriage, Brett and I got used to being separated. We had learned how to translate our love across long distances.

It definitely wasn't my favorite thing, but we had learned to deal with this separation as best we could, as we had many times before. However, I had no practice being separated from my child, and it was a steep learning curve. The longest I had ever been apart from Ransom was for the surgery only weeks before. Now we were delving into the unknown and hard territory of long separation. To say I lived and breathed for those few hours of time with Ransom on the weekends was an understatement. I had nothing to compare with this all-consuming love for my firstborn child, but it was life altering.

Ransom was pretty high maintenance. Everything had to be just so. He was going through that phase where he was constantly asking where everyone in his life was at that moment: "Where's Daddy? Where's Mommy? Where's ..." The list would go on until he had everyone in their spot. Also, he had never been a good sleeper. Everything had to be exactly right for him to even think about sleeping. He had to have his special friends, Bear and Lamb, his bed, his paci, a white noise maker making just the right amount of noise. The room had to have just the right degree of darkness. He would only lie down exactly at his scheduled nap or bedtime, not a minute too late or too early. Then, just maybe, he might just possibly go to sleep.

That day when Ransom arrived for his weekly visit looking flushed and sticky with snot, he asked to climb up next to me on the bed. To my utter amazement, he fell asleep in my arms. I lay there, as still as I possibly could, soaking in the joy of being close to my baby boy. As luck would have it, I really needed to pee, but I didn't want to move. I had missed him so terribly all week, and here he was, his sweaty little curls pushed up on top of my giant belly, breathing deeply. Hard to believe he had ever been small enough to fit in that same belly. He was now so independent and grown up at the ripe old age of two and a half. When I looked at him lying there, I knew he was still my little baby, a baby with a bad cold who needed his Mommy to love on him for a little while. It was a glorious hour of peaceful snuggles, watching his little chest move in perfect little intervals, his little face, calm and sweet. Those gorgeous eye lashes against his intensely chubby cheeks. I sat as still as I could until Ransom woke up and since he was sick, we decided it was best to cut the visit short. Of course, I was sad. Our weekend times together were short enough already.

But I comforted myself by making plans with Amy to have a special dinner. We ordered pizza from a specialty pizzeria near the hospital that would deliver directly to us, and we sat around, waiting for our order. As we waited for our food, we watched my evening nurses do their Tabitha monitoring. I wasn't even that concerned when nurse after nurse started filling up my room fiddling with the monitors. I figured it was just a slow night and they were bored.

Then they asked for my arms and started to look for a vein to start up an IV, "just in case." My veins are particularly difficult when it comes to getting IVs in, and, at one point I had two nurses on each arm trying to find veins. That's four people; but other than the obvious pain of being stuck with multiple sharp objects, I still wasn't too worried. Another nurse, monitor in hand, was searching for Tabitha's heartbeat. She searched and searched, and I waited expectantly. I kept calmly reminding myself of what had happened with Esther only a few weeks before when Tabitha had just moved out of position. Things were going to be just fine, I was sure.

Finally, the nurse found Tabitha's heartbeat. It was slow - so, so slow. I was immediately taken back to the sound of Priscilla's slow, slow heartbeat after the surgery. All of a sudden, everything seemed to stop and the seconds became as slow as Tabitha's little heart, as everyone in the room waited for it to start beating normally. I sat, every muscle tense, in my bed, waiting to see what would happen next. The nurses rushed to call Dr. Sing, who was on call for the weekend. He showed up in his workout clothes, having rushed to the hospital in the middle of moving stuff out of storage and into his new house. Seeing my usually professional doctor standing there in his outside-the-hospital clothes brought the situation home in a way I can't fully describe. He had a life somewhere outside that hospital building, and he'd dropped it suddenly to run to my bedside. He pulled in an ultrasound machine and started checking Tabitha for movements and breathing, making strained small talk with me as we waited to see if Tabitha would pass her tests.

Then Dr. Rivera showed up having come straight from the airport where he was returning from a conference in Chicago. The worry in my heart morphed to full-on fear when he calmly explained they couldn't risk letting Tabitha's heart decelerate so seriously again. If it happened again, I would have an emergency Caesarean that night. It was the night before Tabitha would be officially 28 weeks. It was still dangerous for her to be born that soon, but the doctors felt like it was more dangerous for her heart to continue those decelerations. Her heart was sick. It couldn't be trusted to bounce back on its own. I sat there as the doctors told me they might need to "take Tabitha" that night. When it came time to ask my questions, I just had one:

> "Should I call Brett? Is it serious enough to pay for him to fly here tonight?"
>
> "Call your husband. Get him here."

So I called Brett, and told him to get on a plane and to come as quickly as he could. My heart was racing ninety miles an hour. Having my doctors essentially tell me Tabitha's condition required my husband to take an emergency flight from Georgia put the odds of Tabitha making it through the night inside of me very, very small. The seriousness was finally winning the war over my eternal optimism. I sat in numb shock watching as my dear friend Amy calmly helped a nurses' aide gather up my belongings in preparation for moving out of my current hospital digs. My three weeks-worth of living and gift receiving had resulted in quite a collection in the room, but it couldn't stay. I was officially being wheeled down to labor and delivery and prepped for a C-section. I was so scared.

I knew in my heart of hearts it was not a good time for Tabitha to come, and I was crying out to the Lord to make this all stop. I sent out texts and Facebook messages because all I wanted was prayer and lots of it. I wanted everyone I had ever met or who had ever heard of me or Tabitha to stop everything and *pray*. While it would have been nice to have prayers prayed over me in person, I know the effects of those prayers that came from all over. I got what I wanted: my Facebook timeline from that day shows many of my friends shared our story on their own timelines, and hundreds of people said prayers for Tabitha that night. Entire churches prayed over our baby girl at their Saturday night services. People whom I will probably never meet until heaven prayed over Tabitha that night.

I was wheeled down to labor and delivery and put into the most giant delivery room ever. I mean ever. I have no idea why they even have room options that large, but I guess if your birth plan included a string quartet, your entire extended family, and a chef in the corner running an omelet station, this would be the room you'd chose. I don't know where Beyoncé gave birth, but if she decided to do it in her hometown of Houston, Texas, she could fit her entourage in that room. I didn't have an entourage, so there I was, all alone in a little hospital bed in a sea of emptiness waiting for Amy to arrive with her precariously stacked cart full of all my stuff.

I cried in that big empty room. I had waited through listening to Tabitha's heart beating slower and slower. I waited through my doctors telling me to call Brett. I waited as they wheeled me down the hall to this giant room, but now that I was there, alone for a few seconds as I waited for Amy to catch up, I cried, choking on sobs and powerless to stop what was going on in my own body and what was happening to my sweet baby girl - her body still desperately holding on to life. I tried to continue to pray, to believe in all the prayers of all the people who were praying for us. Yet, I felt nothing but fear. All I could think was, *Where is the Lord's peace now?"*

It was a horrible night. The giant room loomed around me in the semi-dusk. A few lights were left on for the nurses to come check on Tabitha. I was on an IV and had to pee every few minutes, so I had to unhook the monitors, drag my IV wheelie across the giant football field of a room, and go into the equally enormous bathroom to pee. I turned down all medicine to help me sleep because I didn't want a repeat of our previous close call. I had to be coherent. I had to be able to make decisions because there was no guarantee Brett would make it in time to help with those decisions. I lay in the dusky darkness between peeing trips, staring at the monitor tracking Tabitha's heart. It was turned down, supposedly so it wouldn't keep me or Amy awake, but, knowing even the slightest deceleration would call in the cavalry, I was not likely to sleep anyway. As I lay there in such fear and doubt for Tabitha, I pleaded with God to protect my little girl.

Then, as the hours of strain ticked away in that cavernous sterile room, my mind went back to earlier that day. Had it really only been a few hours? It seemed like a lifetime. In my mind I saw Ransom curled into the crook of my arm, sleeping on my belly, content and safe. He was with his Mommy, and it was such a peaceful and beautiful moment. I heard the Lord tell me He was holding Tabitha and me in the same way during that very long night. I might not have felt it completely, but we were there, the two of us, nestled in the arms of Jesus. We were held. Peaceful. Protected. All through the long hours of that night, Tabitha's heart beat steadily on in perfect intervals without a blip or variation

I look back on it now and it is most definitely one of the most miraculous parts of our story - especially knowing what I know now about babies at 28 weeks gestation. We don't know a lot about the hearts of babies at that point because they aren't on heart monitors unless they are already at risk. What we do know is their hearts are still being developed, so even the healthiest of 28-week babies have inconsistencies. Tabitha was not the healthiest. All day her heart had been decelerating more and more until it was happening every few minutes. Yet, suddenly, it shifted to beating perfectly, happily, and steadily for nine hours straight. It was incredible. What I see now more clearly is these kinds of silent miracles happen all the time. Often we are in the midst of crying out to God; *Where is the peace now?* Even then, in the middle of our own fear and doubt, He is working, minute after minute, hour after hour, day after day. He is faithfully performing silent miracles, holding us in His arms.

Amy and I woke up—if we slept at all—the next morning still in our giant room. We never had to go to the operating room for the predicted C-section. Brett arrived from the airport, as did my mom, my sister and my aunt, who was there for the next Abigail-watching-shift. They had all driven through the night to be there for the inevitable birth. Instead, we sat around eating cake my aunt had baked for me. It was a party. A celebration that, against all odds, Tabitha was still in my tummy at 28 weeks. Of course, now that we'd made it so far, it was time for me to take some very literal steps outside the hospital.

Chapter Fourteen

For better or maybe a bit worse for wear, we met our newest and greatest milestone up to that point. When I entered the hospital, a battered and broken 25 weeks pregnant, my doctors said their goal was to get Tabitha and me to 28 weeks. Thanks to God's great mercy, the weeks ticked by and she was still growing inside me. We were both doing so much better. My body was recovering from the surgery that had sent me into early labor, and, more importantly, my mind was beginning to heal too. At least the shocks and stresses of our journey were having less effect on my body giving Tabitha more time to heal in my tummy which was the very safest possible place. That said, when my doctors started talking about discharging me from the hospital, my blood pressure immediately started rising.

When I arrived in the hospital, I was a mess. I was on the verge of labor. I was a bucket of nerves. I was in mourning. I was raw and scared and unsure of what was going to happen to me, to Ransom, and, most importantly, to Tabitha. In the hospital, we came up with a new normal. I no longer had to worry about myself. I lay in bed and had food brought to me three times a day and had unlimited Wi-Fi. It was hard to complain. I no longer had to worry about Ransom's daily care. Though it was difficult having him so far away, we both were used to our routine of visits on the weekends and Facetime every night. I was grateful he had the stability of a routine and had our wonderful family to take care of his daily needs. My time in the hospital was restorative, and I was hesitant to leave my comforting bubble. I rarely left my room. Everything came to me. The farthest I had been from my room, other than going down the hall for ultrasounds, was for a craft time some volunteers put on for the preggo moms on my floor. The thought of walking outside, going into a more demanding environment, seemed beyond my comprehension.

My doctors nixed the idea of me returning to the Humble House. Even though it was close, it was still 30 minutes away on a good day in city traffic. I wouldn't be able to drive myself, so if I went there, I would need someone with me at all times. Their new plan was for me to stay at the Ronald McDonald House down the street from the hospital.

I had no idea what to expect with this new plan, therefore I didn't like it one bit. Unknowns and uncomfortables were not my favorite, and I was stubbornly unhappy about leaving the hospital. Thankfully, God was patient with me and after the scare that sent me briefly to labor and delivery, we were given an extra week in the hospital. Yet again, the perfect person was scheduled for the job of getting me ready to leave. My Aunt Donnave was up for Abigail Duty that particular week.

Aunt Donnave was the ideal person to help me with this mental transition because she had personal experience with the same Ronald McDonald House. She had stayed at this very Ronald McDonald House 25 years before when my cousin had open heart surgery. I was an infant when these events happened, so I hadn't really known much about that time in my aunt's life. Now things had come strangely full circle as Aunt Donnave went with me to one of my fetal cardiology appointments and mentioned names of doctors who had helped my cousin thirty years before. She found out some of them were still around. Donnave was able to speak with authoritative excitement about my time ahead at the Ronald McDonald House. From her I got a glimpse of what I could expect, and it eased some of my fears of the unknown.

At the same time, Donnave also began to prepare me, in a much more physical and practical way, to leave the hospital. She tracked down a wheelchair, put fuzzy slippers on my feet and pushed me out of my hospital room. We went further than I had been in weeks. It was really only to the other side of the building, but it was a huge building, and we might as well have traveled to the other side of the country for the impact it had on me.

The part of Texas Children's Hospital where I had been was aptly named the Women's Pavilion, but my aunt pushed me over a little sky bridge into the full-fledged Children's Hospital. For the first time in a long while, I started to look outward again, and what I saw was life altering. It is a Children's Hospital, known for being one of the best, and those who go there are usually in need of help for the most serious illnesses. It's no stretch to imagine children and their families in such a place are struggling. Seeing children in such extremities of need is incredibly impactful. As Donnave pushed me in the wheelchair, we ran into a lady I had met on my floor who had delivered twins several months early via C-section. She proudly and tearfully showed me pictures of her two baby girls. Barely 2 pounds apiece, the girls were covered in monitors, wires, and tubes that were keeping them alive.

My aunt pushed me around only a small section of the hospital for a half hour, yet I was thoroughly exhausted as though I'd walked through an entire city. As selfish as I am, I might have been too afraid to come out of my hole - a hole I had dug with my own fears and grief. I had been sitting at the bottom of it for several months, protected by the bubble of my hospital room. I'm thankful the Lord was willing to pull me out of that hole and that He used Aunt Donnave to help me realize I was not alone in my fears and grief. So, as I packed up my stuff and moved half a mile down the road to the Ronald McDonald House, I also began my climb out of the hole and up toward the light.

Up until this time in my life, the closest I had ever been to a Ronald McDonald House was a near miss with the plastic collection buckets sticking out of the drive-through wall at my local McDs. Over the next three months that changed drastically as I lived and experienced first-hand what Ronald McDonald House is all about. I soon learned this particular Ronald McDonald House is set up a little bit like a hotel. Rooms are on the upper floors and the bottom floor is made up of large seating areas, the dining room, and kitchen. The kitchen is a large industrial sized kitchen. It is divided into about ten mini kitchens with each equipped with an oven and stove for the use of those living at the house. Residents share duties to keep the main areas clean and are also expected to keep their own rooms clean and tidy.

My room had two queen beds, a set of drawers, a table with two chairs, and a bathroom. If I'd stayed in this kind of hotel room in my normal life, I would have given it about two stars for visual attractiveness. But it was clean and relatively comfortable, and, best of all, it was incredibly cheap. To those families who are already facing insurmountable medical bills and must remain near the hospital indefinitely for treatment, such a place is truly a godsend. Most of the people there were not there for just one or two days. Many families I met had been there for months, some for almost a year, and some were back for a second or third time. Families came from all over the world to receive treatment for their children at the hospitals clustered together in downtown Houston. So many illnesses, so many stories, so many children, all connected by their need for a place to stay, a place to retreat while fighting the battles of a having a sick child.

I definitely stuck out from the crowd, because, other than weekends when Ransom came to visit, I didn't have a child with me, at least not on the outside of my body. Nothing put my own situation in perspective like staying in that place where every one I met was going through the ringer. For the previous weeks, I had been the patient, surrounded by caregivers and friends. Here, I was surrounded by families in crisis, some of them living through their worst nightmare.

For the first week or so at the Ronald McDonald House, I wondered why the atmosphere seemed so unfriendly. After I had been there for a while and recognized what these families were experiencing, I realized they weren't unfriendly. They simply didn't have the energy to reach out to the new girl because they were already using up all their resources. Parents were fighting for their children's health, fearing for the future. The children were using every ounce of energy to heal, often through tremendous suffering and much upheaval. These people did not need to start a conversation with an emotional pregnant woman in the elevator. They were too spent even to return my smiles in the dining room. These were people running on empty and rationing their reserves.

Now that I was out of the hospital, Ransom could actually come stay with me overnight, as long as someone else was there to help me take care of him. The Ronald McDonald House was a great place for him to come because it was made for kids. It had two play areas, tricycles, trucks, and blocks for all. Kid-pleasing events were happening all the time: petting zoos, visits from Cookie Monster, face-painters, balloon artists, and more. Ransom could spend all weekend living it up, sitting in real race cars, chatting with professional basketball players, or playing with therapy puppies. Too bad the kid was only two and wouldn't be able to remember the famous people he met and the fun he had. It was infinitely better than our brief visits back in my hospital room. Yet, no matter how much fun was had, the weekend would inevitably come to an end, and I would face a week ahead without my family. How I missed Ransom and Brett.

One day, after saying goodbye to Ransom and my mom, I was sitting forlornly in the common area. Mom had so sweetly made the long drive to bring him to spend the weekend, and I loved that. Saying goodbye, however, was never easy. I had stopped expecting other residents to speak to me, but that day, a lovely lady sitting next to me in the common area struck up a conversation. I soon learned she was visiting her friend, Jane, whose son, KJ, was receiving treatment for a cancerous brain tumor.

KJ was an eleven-year-old boy from rural Kentucky. He wore the physical battle scars of brain cancer, but his spirit remained unscathed. Cancer treatment can be almost as brutal to the body as the disease it fights. He could have had every reason and excuse to allow those scars to rule his life, but he didn't.

After getting to know KJ and his mom, I sat with them at dinner almost every day. There were days when KJ's treatment left him exhausted and in pain, but he didn't complain. When family and friends called him, he talked to them with incredible maturity - the same with adult volunteers at the RM House. As he spoke to others, I saw him rally right before my eyes. In every conversation, he made people feel special. He helped others see past his suffering because he was able to see past his own suffering. It was one of his gifts.

KJ also had a wonderful sense of humor. His wit was so quick, and he seemed to always look for ways to make light of heavy situations. He did not let his difficulties bog him down, and he wanted to make sure they didn't bog down the people around him either. He exuded hope and peace in a way that was otherworldly. He was the most calm and peaceful person in that place, and he'd be the first to say it was because of Jesus. KJ and his mom were continually sharing and living out their belief that all things were possible through Jesus. I was reminded of Jesus' power because of what I saw Him do in KJ.

In so many ways, KJ was just a typical eleven-year-old boy who was super excited for the newest Star Wars movie coming out and who liked to go to comic book stores to buy a few more Storm Trooper action figures for his collection. He told me he tried to get up early on Saturday mornings to get to the TV room before anyone else so he could watch the cartoons he wanted to see. He loved the breadsticks and pasta at Olive Garden. Sickness was trying to destroy his body, but it couldn't touch his spirit.

KJ, Jane and I became buddies getting through our days in the Bubble for a little over two months. I was so grateful for Jane's friendship during that time. Those two months together often feel much longer to me, especially because of the impact that KJ had on me. I learned, through KJ, that our circumstances do not change who God is. He is still worthy of all our praise and adoration. KJ also taught me that how I behave, how I treat others, is a choice. Even in the midst of personal battles, I can choose to think of others first. With the Lord's help, KJ did that every single day.

So there we were, slugging it out day in and day out, when I met Cindy. I noticed her when she moved in because she too was pregnant. Very pregnant. She would sit for hours in the common room, reading her Bible, rarely looking up, seemingly oblivious to her surroundings. She seemed to wear an invisible "Do Not Disturb" sign. However, one day I decided to try to break through her aura of indifference. I introduced myself, asked her what she was reading, and the ice was broken. We quickly became friends, bonding over our common situation—pregnant mommies worried about our babies—as well as our shared faith in Jesus. I introduced Cindy to Jane and KJ, and we became regular table buddies at dinnertime.

Later, I found out she had been wondering—as I had when I first arrived—why everyone seemed so unfriendly. I wondered how many others had seen her reading and assumed she didn't want to be interrupted. Or how many were too consumed by their own weighty concerns to reach out to support someone else. I also wondered how often, as Cindy sat reading by herself, she had only been pretending to read. When in reality she stared, unseeing, at the pages hoping someone would say a friendly word. Again and again I was learning my first impressions of people were liable to be mistakes - particularly with those who are suffering. At the Ronald McDonald House many were suffering. Outside those walls many are suffering too, and I was learning not to judge people based on first, or even second, impressions.

Each evening our little haphazard crew would gather. Two pregnant ladies, a young boy and his mama, and others who joined us along the way: a young mother with a thick Cajun accent and her three-year-old daughter who came from Louisiana for a kidney transplant; a mom with her two-year-old son who came from Washington state for yet another surgery to help his broken heart. We ate together, enjoying the meals that were often donated for the residents of RM House, and we shared whatever good news we could find. We would try to entice the kids with macaroni and cheese or a yummy dessert. Because of their various treatments and different needs, none of them ever ate much. And we celebrated one another's victories: "Her kidneys have been cleared! We get to go home!" or "The Doctor says the tumor measures a little smaller this month!" or "Cindy had her baby!"

We would mourn too. When I met Cindy, I had learned her

unborn baby was diagnosed with a congenital diaphragmatic hernia, and he would need many extensive surgeries after his birth to have any chance of survival. Remarkably, Cindy's daughter, a happy, healthy toddler, had endured the same rare condition. Cindy had already been through the fight for her daughter's life, and she was back in the battle again. Sadly, after her son was born, he did not fare as well as his sister. When news came that Cindy's baby boy didn't survive his first surgery, I went to my room and cried and cried.

This was not the only mourning I did for others during those months in the Ronald McDonald House. A friend of my family lost her son, only a few years younger than me, in a car accident, leaving behind his own young family. My grandmother, who had been suffering with severe dementia, passed away. Other friends were dealing with miscarriages and struggling marriages, and it seemed everywhere I turned hearts were raw. Or was it my own raw heart that made me more sensitive to the heartbreak around me? At times, it seemed hard to carry the burdens and sadness of this very fallen world. Sometimes people tried to start up conversations or arguments about whether these awful things were sent by God or if He just allowed them to happen. In the midst of those questions, I still had niggling *what ifs* regarding our loss of Priscilla. *What if we'd prayed harder? What if we believed more? What if we'd been better people?*

Questions like this can morph into lies that try to convince me I have power to keep tragedy and suffering at bay. I found no good answers to my *what if* questions because I was asking the wrong questions altogether.

During this season, I read John 9: 1-3, the story of a man who had been blind since birth. The disciples asked Jesus whose sin caused this blindness, the man or his parents. Jesus said it wasn't about sin at all. It was so God could be glorified. Then Jesus healed the man, and everyone was amazed. Glory to God. Mission accomplished. I was comforted by Jesus' statement that the sins of his parents were not the cause of their son's affliction. I could, once and for all, call off the condemnation dogs that hounded me with *what ifs* about the health and lives of our girls. But there was even more to this story. Up until this point, I hadn't thought much about this particular miracle other than, *Yup, there goes Jesus healing someone again!*

This time when I read the story, I paid more attention to the man - blind since birth. This meant he had already been blind for *years*. Years and years and years, so that one day, after a life of hardship and suffering, Jesus would walk by and heal him. If I could ask the blind man, would he say it was worth it? He endured a lifetime of suffering so he could one day be healed by the Savior of the World. His story was then told far and wide during his lifetime and later written down and included in the Word of God. His life of blindness became a testimony of the Lord Jesus Christ.

So often, I am guilty of seeing my life, and the lives of my friends and family, through very limited eyes – my own little human eyes. I want all suffering to stop. Immediately. Especially if it affects me or someone I love. But, every so often, we get a little glimpse of life through Jesus' eyes. He shows me He can use all things to bring glory and honor to God. I bet, one day, when we get to heaven and we run into that once-blind-but-now-he-sees guy, he would say, "Yes, the blindness was worth the healing." He will tell us how loved he felt and the importance of the day he met Jesus. He met his personal Savior in the flesh. The Savior gave him sight - both physically and spiritually.

We can rest on the promise that all the days we spend blind, all the days we suffer injustice, hardship, trials, and heartbreak, all those things will be one day be redeemed. None of our suffering is wasted or purposeless. They will all be made right, and the King of Kings will be glorified.

Chapter Fifteen

During those months in the Ronald McDonald House, the Lord was teaching me a lot about time and His timing. We went back to Dr. Allison, the fetal cardiologist, and she marveled I made it to our appointment. She had not thought I would still be pregnant.

Honestly, neither did we, because every time I had an ultrasound, the technician would measure my cervix. For those not well-versed in birthing terminology, when babies are about to be born, the doctor starts talking about cervix thinning. The cervix is one of the things keeping that baby up inside the uterus. When the cervix starts thinning the barrier between the baby and the outside world is about to become nonexistent. Since I'd essentially gone into labor at 19 weeks, my cervix was already very thin. When the ultrasound techs would measure my cervix—what little was left of it—they would look at me nervously, wondering why I wasn't having a baby right in front of them. Of course, there are a lot of elements that work together to keep a baby in utero. Fortunately for me, and Tabitha, the cervix is just one of the elements. Those first weeks in the hospital when we were shooting for 28 weeks, I would wake up each morning and delight in the miracle of still being pregnant. Each day was a victory: one more day for Tabitha's heart to heal, one more day for her lungs to develop, one more day for her to become stronger and have a better chance at survival. Each day was a gift.

As the "gifts kept on giving," so to speak, I forgot to be grateful. I still knew every day was important, but those days that were so beneficial for Tabitha were more days away from Brett and Ransom, and I missed them horribly. By the beginning of November, Dr. Allison and Dr. Rivera were incredibly optimistic about Tabitha's life and began throwing around numbers like 38 weeks as a possible end goal for the pregnancy. Those weeks—during which I would have to remain close to the hospital in Houston—would keep me away from my family through Thanksgiving, my twenty-ninth birthday, Christmas, and the New Year. Milestones marked away from my home and family.

The separation was wearing, and I had become a hot mess of ungratefulness. As I was preparing for the Christmas season, I read a scripture that spoke directly to me.

But the angel said to him, "Do not be afraid, Zechariah, for your prayer has been heard, and your wife Elizabeth will bear you a son, and you shall call his name John." Luke 1:13 (NIV)

The words, "your prayer has been heard," jumped out from the page at me. Luke also says that Zechariah and his wife Elizabeth were "very old." No doubt they had hoped and prayed for a child, but perhaps hope had faded as their hair grew gray and their joints stiffened. We don't know if Zechariah and Elizabeth had given up, but the Lord had not forgotten. To Him, that prayer was as fresh as the day it was first offered.

I found such comfort in this reminder: even when I lack the faith to keep praying, or to believe in God's ability to answer, or when my heart is too grieved and hurt to put my longings into words, God has not forgotten my prayers or the desires of my heart. He hears them, and He never forgets. When I think of the suffering this world holds in unspeakably large quantities, I must remember the Lord's promises stand firm. Our prayers are heard.

In my journals from those months in the Ronald McDonald House, these verses are scrawled over the pages…

For nothing will be impossible with God. Luke 1:37 (ESV)

He will wipe away all tears from their eyes, and there will be no more death or sorrow nor crying nor pain. All these things are gone forever. Rev. 21:14 (TLB)

Every valley shall be lifted up, and every mountain and hill will be made low, the uneven ground shall become level, and the rough places made smooth. Isaiah 40:4 (NIV)

Do not be afraid, for I have ransomed you. I have called you by name;
you are mine. Isaiah 43:1 (TLB)

Even in my own faithlessness, my own inability to keep my eyes
on the prize, God was still using His word to remind me He
would remain faithful.

On many days I was just not up for faithfully praying as I
should. Instead, I would complain. Sometimes I complained
about something valid, like how I missed getting to sit across
from Brett in the morning, drinking coffee together and talking
about our day. For that matter, I missed enjoying coffee since it
gave me awful indigestion during my last trimester. So, even that
part of my dream scenario was a bust. Other times I showed off
my spoiled nature and complained about truly inconsequential
things like the terrible Wi-Fi connection at the RM House.

One thing I really missed was the familiarity of my home,
especially during the holidays. I love decorating for the holidays.
Holiday traditions are in my blood. When I was growing up, if
we did something fun on Thanksgiving Day even one time, the
whole family would immediately dub it "tradition," and we'd
have to do it again and again and again for the rest of our lives.
"Tradition!" (Shout it out, like Papa from *Fiddler on the Roof.*) But
there I was stuck in the most untraditional place of my life. This
was one holiday season my whole family would agree they *never*
wanted to do again.

On Thanksgiving, and again at Christmas, we reserved multiple
rooms in a hotel in Houston, and my wonderful family came

and spent time with us. It was a merciful change of scenery, and, for just a brief moment, I could feel like a normal pregnant woman. Yet it was still so far from the typical family-at-home holiday atmosphere I craved. On Christmas morning, Brett and I woke up with Ransom in our Ronald McDonald room and watched him open his presents on one of the queen-sized beds. Surrounded by suitcases and outdated hotel bedspreads, it was not a very picturesque Christmas by Abigail's unattainable "White Christmas" standards, but my mother-in-law had given us a tiny decorated tree to give us a little bit more Christmas cheer.

We moseyed downstairs for Christmas Day Brunch with Ransom, the only one of us who had the luxury of staying in his pjs. He sat at the piano "helping" a gentleman play Christmas carols, and then another volunteer made Ransom a balloon dog. Yes, despite my bad attitude, there was much to be grateful for that holiday. Kind volunteers gave up their Christmas day to make ours brighter. We were together, having made it through many difficult months. Tabitha was still moving around in my tummy, getting healthier by the day. In spite of so much to be thankful for, I was impatient to move past this whole season of our lives. At times, I was decidedly ungrateful for the many ways we had been blessed, but God was still faithful to our prayers we prayed over Tabitha's heart, over her life.

He was still being faithful to our heart cry and to what was truly important. Turns out, Abigail's idea of a perfect Christmas was *not* important. And, truth be told, I don't think I've *ever* had a

Christmas that completely fulfilled all my crazy expectations. No, the Lord knew what was truly important. So often, when we're in the desert places of our lives, those days between, all we care about is getting out of the desert, getting past the awfulness of waiting. We grow tired of waking up each morning and looking expectantly to heaven to sustain us. Like the children of Israel, we want to be self-sustaining. We want to wake up already knowing we'll have what we need. Yet, God knew we needed our time in the desert to learn fully and completely know who is in charge.

The weeks passed: 35, 36, 37. By then, Brett was on block leave, meaning he had extended time away from work. Blessedly, this coincided with the holidays, and now he and Ransom could stay with me while we waited for Tabitha's birth. I was so much happier. Like a typical child, after I got my first wish of having our little family back together, I immediately had a new one. I wanted to be together at home. Tabitha was past the danger zone, and our doctors were optimistic about her heart. I spent New Year's Eve climbing up and down the stairs of the Ronald McDonald House willing my little girl to be born.

My motives for wanting to go into labor weren't entirely selfish: Dr. Rivera was worried about the state of my body, particularly my placenta, and wanted to induce labor at 38 weeks, if I didn't go into labor by then. The thought of pumping my body full of labor inducing drugs after all we had been through to prevent labor didn't seem like the right ending to Tabitha's birthing story. Not to mention the irony of the word "induce" being part of the vocabulary of this story at all. Of course, as an English major, I love irony. It beats the lousy math we started with. So, there I was, stomping up and down the stairs, trying my hardest to try to get her out. After all we'd been through, she didn't seem to want to come at all. Or so I thought.

We spent the early days of January as a little family of three: going to museums, walking to parks, enjoying uninterrupted time together. Brett and I would put Ransom to bed and then sit outside our room, where there was a little seating area with a couch, listening to the baby monitor and willing Ransom to go to sleep. As I said, he was never an awesome sleeper. His latest delaying tactic was to request endless drinks of water. Brett and I would sit on the couch playing a game or reading out loud to one another.

This did much for my heart - not the two-year-old who was part camel, but the time spent with my husband. Playing games, reading to each other, these were the moments I had missed the most. We started reading out loud on our honeymoon, and it has always been one of my most treasured times with him. What a sweet change from my weeks of mindless binge-watching *Gossip Girl* until I was too tired to keep my crying eyes open.

Two days before Tabitha was scheduled to be induced, we were having yet another come-to-Jesus moment with Ransom over his nightly death-inducing thirst, and I was eating the most heavenly chocolate cake known to man. Seriously. This piece of cake was the size of my head. It was soft and fluffy and thick and rich. All at the same time, you ask? Oh, yes! It was magical – the most chocolaty wonderfulness ever. One piece cost something insane like ten dollars and worth every penny. I still dream about that cake. It was from a place called The Chocolate Bar in the part of downtown Houston called Rice Village. (This is me giving a shout out to that store in my book, hoping maybe they'll give me unlimited chocolate cake forever. A girl can dream.)

Other than the magical chocolate cake, it was a normal night in the Ronald McDonald House. Families were slowly making their way home from the hospital for the night, many of them mentally and physically exhausted from being the support system their child needed all day, every day. Brett and I sat on the couch outside our room speaking to those we had come to know over my months there. In a weird sort of way, this place was becoming home. I both loved and hated that fact. Finally, Ransom fell asleep, Brett and I finished our book—we had been reading *Heidi* by Joanna Spyri—and we took ourselves to bed. Sometime in the middle of the night, I woke and sat straight up, wondering if I had wet the bed. Fortunately for my self-respect, I discovered my water had broken. At first just enough had leaked out to get me out of bed to investigate, and then a lot more gushed out to confirm that, yes, this wasn't a weird chocolate-induced dream.

The clock said 3:30 a.m. I texted my parents and my sister, so they could start getting ready for the drive from Nacogdoches. Then I calmly woke up Brett and told him what had happened.

He called his mom, and we implemented the plan we had argued about a few days before: the what-to-do-with-sleeping-Ransom-if-I-go-into-labor-in-the-middle-of-the-night plan. I didn't think Ransom needed to be awakened and dragged to the hospital at 4 a.m. to wait until family arrived. This seemed like my worst nightmare. In my limited I-have-only-had-one-child world, I did not, and I repeat, did not want to wake up my toddler. I mean, this kid took a trillion years to fall asleep, and once he was awake again? Lord help you; he would not fall back asleep. Ransom came into the world with a terrible fear that if he fell asleep he would miss something, and he had been fighting sleep ever since. So there we were, in the wee hours of the morning, trying to decide what to do about Ransom.

We discovered one of the moms at the Ronald McDonald House, who was apparently unable to sleep that night, sitting outside her room playing on her iPad. We recruited her as an emergency babysitter, armed her with our baby monitor, and headed off to the hospital. All this was done calmly and without much drama, because even though my water had broken, I wasn't having any contractions. In fact, when I called the hospital saying I was coming in, the resident on duty was incredulous.

"Well, come on in and *if* your water has *actually* broken..." she began, to which I kind of laughed because I still don't see how I would mistake something like that. She was apologetic, and told me she'd delivered four babies that night and had just gone to sleep - like any of that affected my water breaking. Fortunately for her, I hadn't had any contractions yet so I wasn't annoyed. Instead I texted Dr. Rivera because he was the one we really needed to be there with us. With Ransom taken care of until my parents arrived, I turned all my worry toward Tabitha. Now that the day was finally here, I began to worry about actually giving birth to Tabitha, and, yes, to Priscilla, too.

One of the things we discussed as we got closer to Tabitha's birth was the undeniable fact that Priscilla would be born at the same time. All those weeks Tabitha had been growing and getting bigger, Priscilla had been next to her - the still and tiny baby stuck at the moment in time when her little heart stopped beating. She, too, was waiting to be born. Brett and I had already made some arrangements to have her remains cremated, and we were asked if we would like to see Priscilla before she was taken away.

Here's where I hesitate in our story. I hesitate to talk about what we decided because one thing we learned during this whole time in our lives is people grieve differently. If someone who is also grieving reads this, I do not want my message to be that we did the "right thing." I know how much hurt and confusion this can cause for those who are already dealing with so much. I learned this early, soon after we lost Priscilla, when I received an unsolicited email from someone telling me why I absolutely had to hold her little body in my arms before letting her go. This person told me I would regret it for the rest of my life if I didn't. They cited a bunch of websites on grief and sent me to several forums of women who had lost babies in similar circumstances.

As soon as I read this email, I immediately started to feel guilty. Because, as it turned out, I didn't think I *could* hold my dead baby girl. I was certain it would break me into a million little pieces.

At the time, I was already struggling a great deal seeing her little lifeless body repeatedly on ultrasounds. In my heart, every time I saw her still little body, all I could think was how I wished for the bouncing, moving Priscilla we had first fallen in love with during the first half of my pregnancy. I wanted to focus on those memories. I wanted that to be what I thought of when I thought of Priscilla. It hurt that, every time I shut my eyes, I saw her lifeless body on the black and white ultrasound screen. I didn't think I could handle the flesh and blood version.

Others' reasons and opinions were seeping into my own, and I was beyond confused. Many people have very solid and valid reasons for holding their babies when they are born without life. I completely support the reasoning for their choice. I truly hope it helps them to heal. As for me, once I realized I could not do it myself, I started to feel guilty. I worried Priscilla would not feel as loved if I didn't hold her at least once. This, of course, is silly. Priscilla was already with Jesus having a grand ol' time in heaven where there is no sadness or lack of trust in a mother's love. I'm convinced that all we will know and care about in heaven is God's love.

Our decision would not be about Priscilla's needs. They were all met in Jesus. Our decision was very much about us and how we grieve. After some time, I decided I would knit baby blankets for *both* my girls. When they were born, they would each be wrapped in a blanket I knitted especially for them. Whether they were present in their bodies or not, my baby girls' outward, earthly selves would be wrapped in my love. Dwelling on those happy, hopeful memories of Priscilla before she passed away while I knitted her blanket was exactly what I needed. Our grieving process would be long, confusing, and hard, and would be unique to me and to Brett. No two people are the same in how they grieve, and I hope I will always be sensitive to the needs of others when they are grieving in their own personal ways. The unintended backlash of this well-meaning advice revealed to me how my own opinions could get in the way of understanding the actual needs of those around me.

As we prepared to go to the hospital, I was concerned for both my girls, and I made sure their little blankets were packed in my overnight bag. I began to get mentally ready for Tabitha's birthday. In my mind, Priscilla's birthday will always be in August when she went to be with Jesus. It was in those moments that her life truly began. Now I turned my full attention to Tabitha, praying that when she was born, her heart would be healthy. All her latest EKGs pointed to the positive, but we had been told there was a chance something might be wrong with our little miracle baby that tests could not catch. My mind couldn't help drifting back to that conversation with Dr. Whom-I-never-saw-again and his laundry list of possible problems our little girl might have. After I was signed into labor and delivery, I was hooked up to a monitor. I sighed with relief when we saw

Tabitha's heart was beating strong with no signs of distress.

About that time, we got a call from our last-minute sitter at the Ronald McDonald House, saying Ransom had woken up. Brett went back to wait for my parents' arrival, hoping to get Ransom back to sleep since it was only around 5 a.m.

By the time Brett returned around 6:30 with my Mom and Anna, I was experiencing painful contractions but was still able to talk through them. I was surprised to find I was already dilated to seven centimeters. Even though things were going so smoothly, I asked for an epidural. Delivering two babies, although Priscilla would be small, would be easier with drugs, I was sure. Anna, who had a very fast delivery only months before, pushed the nurses to hurry up the process of getting the epidural, knowing my pain level was increasing, and the intervals between my contractions were steadily decreasing. By the time I got the epidural, the anesthesiologist warned me it probably wouldn't be in full effect before I delivered. I was in more and more pain, and the nurses were discussing bringing the anesthesiologist back in when I told them they had better check me again before doing anything. Sure enough, I was a fully dilated at 10 centimeters. Dr. Rivera had not yet arrived, so I had to work hard to not push until he got there. He made it, and I am so glad. It was very important to me to have Dr. Rivera deliver the girls. Just a little side note: it's incredibly hard to "hold in" a baby.

Within five hours of my water breaking, we were holding our

baby Tabitha. I couldn't help but think of the stark contrast from my first delivery with Ransom. His labor had lasted for *days*. Really, the differences were too many to count. With Ransom, I was so concerned with privacy and preserving the intimacy of my labor. I wanted only the midwife and Brett in the room with me. Now here I was, with two doctors, their attending nurse, two other nurses on one side of me, Brett and my mom on the other, plus a good eight people who were the nurses and doctors there to assess Tabitha after her birth. I did not begrudge one person in that room. Each was important to me.

In the same way I had learned through hard experience that all grief is different. I was learning every birth is special and different, too. I now try to be as supportive as possible of all the ways mothers decide to bring their children into the world. As long as it will mean a happy and healthy mommy and baby at the end of it, a mother should do what makes her comfortable.

Soon after Tabitha was born, Priscilla was also born. After asking Dr. Rivera about her condition and considering his advice, Brett decided he too didn't think he could see her. Twenty more weeks inside the womb had significantly altered Priscilla's little body, and she wasn't the same little girl she had been when we first lost her. I was thankful she was wrapped in the special blanket I made for her and, while her body may have gone through the ringer, she herself was already in a far more beautiful place. It was a solid reminder that our earthly bodies are temporary vessels, and we shouldn't get too attached to them. However, I was very thankful for the pictures my doctors were able to take of Priscilla during the surgery on her last full day of life.

I asked Brett, several years later, if he had any regrets about his decision not to see and hold Priscilla's body. Brett smiled a sad, slow smile. "No," he said. "Our little girl was already with her Heavenly Father."

The longest half-second in the world was the half-second after Tabitha was born and before she let out a cry. I still had so much fear wrapped up in her birth. It was terribly hard to have her immediately whisked to the other side of the room for assessment, but I was grateful we had a team of doctors there to check her over. When we did finally get to hold her, she opened her eyes and looked up at Brett and me for the longest time. We fell in love again. Tabitha Lorien, our little miracle baby was born at 9:33 a.m. on January 5th, 2013, weighing 5 lbs. 7 oz., and was 18 inches long.

When Ransom was born, and the nurse called out his birth time of 14:21, we immediately looked at each other and knew we were claiming John 14:21 as Ransom's birth verse. With Tabitha we once again found ourselves in John. This time the verse was 9:33.

It was no accident that this is the story of the blind man, the same one that had spoken to me earlier in my pregnancy. Here, at the end of the story, in verse 33, the man who now can see thanks to Jesus, testifies to the religious leaders that someone who could heal his blindness *must be* God. As we looked down at our perfect little girl lying in our arms, we acknowledged that even a room full of doctors couldn't heal Tabitha's heart completely. Even our doctors and all their medicine could not keep her in utero full term or give her a perfectly healthy uncomplicated delivery. Only someone who "must be the Christ" could do all of that.

Chapter Sixteen

The day of Tabitha's birth, when our many visitors had all dispersed for a few minutes and even Brett had stepped out to run an errand, I lay in bed staring at our long-prayed-for little one. She had nestled into my arm after eating, and I was just sitting there thanking God for her life, when the nurses' aide came in to take my blood pressure. As the aide went about her procedures, she said, "It feels good in here." I said something about how the air conditioner was on, but she said it was something more. She looked down at us and said, "It feels peaceful."

She was so right. After nights when I used up entire boxes of tissues, after being separated from my family for four months, we were at peace. We were about to see the fruition of the Bible promise that the Lord would *"restore that which the locust have*

153

taken." Joel 2:25

We spent so many months focused on keeping Tabitha in, and then the last few weeks—which felt like months to me—eager to get Tabitha out. All the months in the hospital had been focused most importantly on having a healthy baby. It was truly an all-consuming desire for those closest to Tabitha, but real life had continued on around us during those months. Ransom had grown and matured. He had grown more independent, and had developed a huge vocabulary for such a little guy. He made conversation like an adult. While in Nacogdoches with my parents, he attended preschool which helped my family with his daily care. From my hospital bed, I watched videos and saw pictures of his very first day of school and his first Christmas program, mourning the firsts I had missed with Ransom and could never get back. And yet I delighted in the incredible bond that was created between Ransom and my dad during their many days together. It is a bond that remains to this day.

Brett's career was undergoing changes, too. Although I was holed up in a hospital in another state for months on end, our bills kept coming. Brett had to keep going to work. I mentioned before his job was very demanding, and it was. In fact, it was very much the most demanding job he had so far in the military, and there was a lot riding on it. His performance in this job was key to his long-term goals. He was in an environment that told him every single day "The Job is Life." The very culture of the workplace demanded to be priority one - above family, above all. The mantra was that this job was an honor to have; those who were lucky enough to hold the position were to be envied; they should hold on to its power and prestige as long as possible. That was the environment in which my husband worked.

Yet, when Brett was only a year and a few months into this position, as I sat in the Ronald McDonald House and he was far off in Georgia, Brett took action on his convictions and requested to be relieved of his position. He wanted to put his family first, before the United States Army, before his career success, before any achievements the world considered success.

It's hard to explain what those hard days in between Priscilla's death and Tabitha's birth had taught me about my husband because I'd have to describe the long hours, the pressure from those above him, and the pressure he put on himself. I'd have to explain what all those late night phone calls were about, and how many weekend dates were spoiled by an urgent call requiring his immediate attention. There is so much I'd have to put into words. So, instead, I'll just say: My husband is strong. My husband is infinitely caring. My husband is full of integrity. My husband is incredibly humble.

I know these things to be true because I've seen him go without food, without sleep, without rest, for the sake of his men. On top of that, in those months after the surgery, I saw him up his game by adding the craziness that was our personal life. For a solid month, he came home from his 24/7/365 job to take care of Ransom and our home when I was unable to do anything. Then I saw him drop everything, leaving in the middle of a training exercise, to fly to Houston with me for the sake of our twins. He mourned the loss of a daughter and returned to his job in Georgia with scant hours in between. For two months, he traveled back and forth, usually via red-eye flights, between Georgia and Texas, doing more than one person really ever should. He aged before my eyes.

Although you'd think it would be a relief to walk away from a job that forced him to burn the candle at both ends, and stick a wick in the middle as well, I knew it was hard for Brett to give it up. He had worked incredibly hard to gain that position, and leaving it early was a huge sacrifice of self because I know one more thing: my husband is a perfectionist, and he hated to let go of all the things he'd been working on for those 14 months.

I am blessed—beyond grateful—for a husband who puts me and our children above the temporary things of this life. It didn't take long to see how the decisions we made during that season of our lives affected our future. Because Brett left that job when he did, he was able to put in for a new job, one that would move us to San Antonio, Texas. God had already been speaking to our hearts about moving to San Antonio long before I got pregnant with the twins. At the time, we had no idea how we would be able to stay in the army and move there because, as far as we knew, there was no position in Brett's career field there. However, when the army was making Brett's next assignment, they took into consideration Tabitha's possible heart problems, which meant sending us to a medically strong location - like San Antonio. Three months after Tabitha was born, the army sent us to Texas.

However, Brett's decision to put family before career had consequences. A few years later, when he was passed over for promotion, he left active duty and was hired as a civilian for the exact same job. We were able to make the transition to civilian life with hardly a bump in the road.

Within a few paragraphs, I can write how the events of those months—our day between—impacted our future for the better. Sadly, we don't have such foresight when we are in those difficult moments. Sacrificing a career without knowing the outcome takes an amount of faith and conviction that I am thankful my husband has. He was willing, in those hard days between, to love us as Christ loves the church. He chose the Lord's direction for our life together and laid down many of his own dreams in the process. Yet the Lord has been faithful and worked out so much of our story for our good.

But, when Tabitha was born in Houston, we were still stationed at Fort Benning, and the path of Brett's career was still unclear. We continued to put one foot in front of the other believing God's path was the best one - wherever it took us.

One important step was Tabitha's very last EKG to test her heart before she could be officially released from the hospital. I was in bed still recovering from delivery, but Brett stood beside Tabitha's bassinet as the doctors struggled to get our wiggly little girl, screaming at the top of her lungs, to be still long enough to get through the procedure. Brett snapped a few pictures and tried to help the attendants keep Tabitha calm. In a few minutes it was all over. The whole thing was in stark contrast to past EKGs, where everyone in the room was solemn and still, where the procedure had taken almost an hour to perform, where we'd seen images of a heart in serious danger. This EKG gave the medical proof to what we had already felt and what our doctors had suspected: Tabitha's heart was perfect. I sent the picture Brett had taken during the procedure out into the world of social media proclaiming what God had done. Tabitha was healed without a shadow of scientific doubt.

However, it seemed our penchant for drama hadn't quite ended. When Tabitha went in for her one week doctor's appointment to be cleared to fly home, she was instead diagnosed with jaundice. Because of our unique situation, being out of state and away from home, the doctors decided the best thing to do was admit Tabitha into the neonatal intensive care unit— NICU—for some phototherapy to treat the jaundice. Oh, how mundane it seems in comparison to what could have been if her heart had remained damaged. Yet, the idea of having her in the NICU at all broke my very hormonal heart. Tears leaked from my eyes against my will, and I questioned God as to why He would make us go through this after we had already been through so much. *Couldn't we just go home? Couldn't we just forget this struggle had ever happened?*

A few hours later, as we were settled into our corner of the lowest level NICU watching Tabitha bask in the blue glow of her tanning bed, I was reminded of the trip I had taken to this same NICU months before. My doctor had prescribed me a tour of the facility, so I would be familiar with everything when Tabitha was born. All indications were she would need an extended stay in the NICU while she had her first heart surgery or, at the very least, was observed while her vital organs had more time to develop. On that tour, I walked through the vast ward with only the dim lighting and beeping monitors disturbing the hushed rooms. My nurse/guide whispered to me about various procedures and rules that would more than likely become our normal in the coming months. I had seen glimpses of tiny little babies hooked up to countless monitors and machines and wondered what their stories might be. I tried not to think of Tabitha in those same little beds. And now here we were.

There was Tabitha under the blue lights, and other than a little yellowish tint to her skin and the tininess of her stature, she was perfect. We would be out of the NICU in 24 hours. The stark contrast to what could have happened there versus what did happen was overwhelming. I wanted to move on, slam the door on those past 6 months of our lives, but the Lord was telling me we still had some work to do. Healing, yes, there would need to be a lot of that, but also there would need to be sharing. We would need to share what the Lord had done for us. We would need to look what *had* been, what *could* have been, and what *was*. We were to proclaim that our Lord was good through it all. Sometimes it would be hard - like reliving our loss of Priscilla in order to tell her story. Sometimes it would be inconvenient – like staying in an uncomfortable armchair in a NICU all night.

Nevertheless, it would be glorious to proclaim what the Lord had done for us.

Like any new mother, I counted all Tabitha's fingers and toes. During this motherly inspection I noticed a little dimple directly over her heart. At first, I thought it was a wrinkle and would fade soon, but it didn't fade. In fact, it stuck around all through her first year. Tabitha turned out to be a very roly-poly baby, so I wondered if the little dimple would disappear with her rolls. But it only got more pronounced. As she grew, and her rolls faded away, the little mark remained. When I asked her pediatrician about it, they just brushed it off as an odd birthmark, but I knew better. I knew it deep in my soul. The little dimple right over her heart is where the Lord touched her when He healed her heart.

An EKG that shows clearly what had been but is no longer there; a trip to the NICU that reveals what could have been but wasn't - an unexplainable little dimple marking the place of healing. These signs and wonders helped me grasp the reality of what had happened to us. We would never be the same, and Tabitha's life would continue to tell the story of a God who heals.

Chapter Seventeen

After Tabitha's brief stay in the NICU, we were finally able to return to Georgia. We had been in Houston exactly 108 days. I know the precise number of days because of another object lesson, another reminder of the One who numbers my days. As we were flying out of Houston, I took a picture of Ransom looking out the window of the plane. It was a repeat of a picture I took of him looking out the airplane window as we flew into Houston months before. I added that picture of Ransom to a project I had been working on while I was in Houston. I got an idea, while I was whiling away my hours in the hospital for a month, to document each day with a picture. I posted the pictures on Instagram with a count up of Tabitha's life thus far. At the time we were mildly obsessed with her fetal age, to say the least. Then, I decided to make a wall poster for Tabitha's room, using all of the pictures combined – a documentation of our journey during the time while our family was divided.

I started my project by making a blank image on Photoshop. Almost haphazardly, I picked a size: 18 by 24 inches. Then, I took the Instagram pictures I had up to that point and reduced them to 2 inch squares. I continued to take photos each day, ending with the flight out of Houston. At the end of our journey in photos, it turned out like this: The first picture is of Ransom on the plane on our way to Houston - a fitting beginning. The last picture is Ransom on the plane leaving Houston. I did not miss a day or do multiple pictures for any day.

The 18 by 24 poster was the correct size—to the day—of when we would leave. A couple of times, when I was adding my picture for the day, I had pondered what I would do with the blank space at the end, because I just didn't see how I'd possibly fill up the poster. I knew I wanted to have the two airplane pictures as bookends. I had come up with some options to make it aesthetically pleasing if Tabitha arrived at, say, 35 weeks, or 36, or 37. None of that happened. When she was finally born, and our flights were booked home, I counted my days and realized that the 108 two-by-two-inch slots would exactly hold the photos for my 108-day sojourn. It was a prophetic hint of the length of our journey. Crazy, huh? Or maybe not crazy at all.

In the same way, it was no accident the Lord died one horrible Friday, left an awful and empty day between, then came back to life on Sunday. Our own seasons and days between are just as numbered. They, too, are not haphazard. Sometimes we find ourselves in horribly hard times, dark days that seem to spill endlessly into more dark days. Yet, we must know all our seasons have a last day. We may not know when it will be, but rest assured the Lord has a day in mind, and it has already been formatted into place. So, hold on. In the same way He has planned out our days, He's also going to be there for each and every one of them.

Our lifelong wall collage, with its good and bad days juxtaposed next to one another, showing victories and struggles and life in all its little and big milestones, has its very own departure photo at the end, ready to go. We're filling in collages every day, and even hard ones like mine have an end. Whatever the season, those little picture squares are a challenge. Fill them with pictures that are worthy. My own collage has a picture of my iPad showing that I watched the entire series of 30 Rock while on bed rest, so clearly I'm one to talk. But it also has photos of people, reminding us of the relationships that got us through, that changed and challenged us. It shows pictures of ultrasounds and miracles, of hard days and Bible promises. No two days are the same. We've got a wonderful God who is ready and willing to help us fill in those pictures and create the perfect wall art for our lives. I'm so thankful to have this collage to look at and remember that, even in a salty-tear-stained way, those 108 days made us better. And also that they came to an end.

As that season ended, a new one began. A much more typical one: a new baby, a toddler, and a cross-country move. We reveled in these things because they were so normal. For awhile everything seemed easier in comparison to what we had been through. Brett's working late? No problem! At least we got to see him. Baby kept me up all night? Ha! How wonderful that we *have* a baby and a healthy baby! We were a regular Pollyanna crew, but even we would lose sight of how lucky we were at times. For me, the hardest times were Tabitha's baby milestones. They were hard because, as I celebrated her, I simultaneously mourned the loss of Priscilla.

I thought I had done most of my grieving during the first few months after Priscilla passed away, but I know now I saved a bit of my mourning for later. Maybe there is no time limit on grief. I just have to acknowledge it when it comes. Brett and I would talk about how Priscilla would have looked like Tabitha, and we would make bad jokes about how the world just probably couldn't have handled twice as much cuteness. In reality, though, it hurt. It hurt when I saw twins in the grocery store. It hurt when Tabitha rolled over for the first time, and we cheered for her. I would catch myself wondering if Priscilla would have been an early or late roller. Some things became less acutely painful with time, but others didn't.

With each of my children I tried to write them a letter every month, sharing their accomplishments and sweet antidotes. When Tabitha was 3 months old, I wrote her my usual monthly letter. That month, I also felt the need to write one for Priscilla:

Dear Priscilla,

Your sister is 3 months old today, and that's when I mark things like how much she's grown and what she's learning and doing. It is days like this that make me miss you the most. You see, when you went to be with Jesus, before you could even make it outside to meet us, I knew that you were going to a place that would be without pain and sorrow. By going there before you were born, you would miss out on some awful things like pimples, heartbreak, bad hair days, traffic jams, hunger, bullies, taxes, sickness, suffering, and sin. All these things you might just have in life, but a Mama never wants them for her child. And, in this way, I was able to comfort myself when we lost you.

But when I look at your sister, rock her and see her little grin, I think about her future life. I think about all the days her life will have. Days she feels beautiful, days she feels smart, a day she knows Jesus loves her and that she wants a relationship with Him, days when she finds purpose in her life, a day when she finds someone who loves Jesus too and who will love her above all others, a day when she might marry such a person, days she gets to meet her own children - physical or spiritual, a day when she sees beauty in life. As her mother, I look forward to getting to celebrate with her on such days. It makes my heart hurt that I will not get to do the same with you.

It hurt my heart when I hung Tabitha's baby picture on the wall last night, and it was virtually identical to Ransom's newborn picture. Identical. In some ways, I get to see your face every day in my other babies, and yet I still long for yours! Strange. But then when I do start to feel sad about all you are missing, I hear a little whisper in my heart. It reminds me heaven is not just the absence of bad things; it is also the very fullness of all good things! You, my dear, are both beautiful and smart every single day. You also know Jesus in a way even your Mama doesn't understand, but I do envy! You also are not alone in that love, but are enjoying the great cloud of witnesses as the Bible calls them, young and old, but all ageless in heaven. You are living in a world of true love.

So where does that leave us, your parents? Your sister, sadly, will miss the joys of having you as an earthly sister. Where does it leave us? Well, I've thought about it, and I think your absence from our lives has left a hole. A hole that must be filled with either grief, pain, and despair or, hope, faith, and conviction. It is my job to fill that hole, and losing you has made me choose how I'd fill it all over again. It has made me look harder at my take on reality.

Thank you for giving me surer footing on which I choose to stand. Thank you for giving me legitimate ties to heaven even now. Thank you for your little life that spent twenty-one weeks with your sister and me. One day we will celebrate the life you're living now, together with Jesus.

But until then, know that I love you,
Your Mommy

I wrote that letter as we traveled from Georgia to Texas to start a new season - a season that would begin with much needed healing for our family. This letter was the start. With tears streaming down my face, I had to acknowledge both the joy of the truth and the sadness of it as well. In different ways, each of our girls had taught me that. Just as the Lord had completely healed Tabitha's heart, I knew He was promising to do the same with my heart as well. It might take all the way until I get to heaven, but He will do it because He never gives up on us and He never stops working.

He also answers every prayer. This includes one I wrote for Priscilla when we first chose to name her for a woman who spent her life sharing the good news of Jesus. I still believe Priscilla will spread the Gospel. Its truths were written upon her life, and those truths have not changed. I am learning the responsibility is on me, on Brett, and all those who loved her, to share the Gospel in her stead. We will tell her story. We will tell all the Lord has done. It may indeed be a story of encouragement and a story of teaching and a story of service. No prayer goes unanswered. Our prayer for Priscilla is no exception.

Acknowledgments

This book would not have been possible without the love of Jesus Christ who died and conquered death for me. It was that same Jesus who performed true and unexplainable miracles from 2012-2013 through the lives of my daughters. All I did was try to write them all down.

You would think it hinted at being almost cliché and expected to thank Jesus Christ first in one's book acknowledgments, but how untrue. Instead, to thank Him first is the very least I could do. This book is but a tiny speck of an offering to a Savior of whom I do not deserve to speak, and yet who chose to come to this earth, live a beautiful and perfect life, performing incredible miracles and showing love to all people, sinners and outcasts and everyone in between. He then chose to give up His own life. He was killed on a cross—though He did not deserve it—and in His death He gave each of us a chance for a true and lasting life with Him. After three days, He rose from the grave and He now sits on the throne of all heaven and earth. One day He will return and make all things as they should be. Perhaps you do not already have a personal relationship with Jesus Christ. Perhaps you read this book and wonder what in the world I am talking about when I say things like, "and Jesus spoke to me," or "I prayed." Perhaps you read the hard things that happen to our family and wonder how we can still call Jesus "good." Perhaps you are wondering how you could ever trust this Jesus I talk about when your own hurts and messy life seem to be all consuming. Yet, maybe you know deep down that you'd like to finally hand your heart over to the One who can be trusted to bring life where there is death, bring hope where there is disappointment, and love where there is despair. If so, then please, please do not stop digging deeper into finding out who Jesus really is. Get a Bible. Start to read it for yourself (Start with the book of Luke. It's my favorite.) Find someone who you can trust to read it with you. And when you're ready, just pray. He will listen. He will answer.

Thank you to my wonderful husband, Brett. You are my perfect partner, greatest cheerleader, kindest critic, and most patient supporter. Without a word of complaint, you allowed me to relive your hardest days and air our dirty laundry for the world to see. I could not have written this book without you as my right hand. To our children Ransom, Tabitha and Justice who all had to bear with me being a less than stellar mother when I was writing and could hear absolutely nothing outside of the words in my own head. I love you so much it hurts.

Thank you to my family who allowed their own lives to be all consumed by ours during that hard year. Thank you to my parents, Jeff and Leabeth Abt, who along with all that you did for us, dropped everything and took on a two-year-old along with your other full-time jobs. While your roles in this book might seem minor to the casual reader, your impact is probably a book unto itself. Your selflessness is beyond words. Mama and Papa, you are the greatest example of love I could ever have. Thank you to Brett's mom, Mary Vermeulen, who also helped watch Ransom in any free time she had, and who braved the difficulty of long trips in the car to allow me to see Ransom on the weekends when my parents couldn't make the trip. To my sister, Anna Middlebrook: Thanks to you I went well over my cell-phone minutes almost every month during that season. You are the best free therapy a girl could ask for and the only person I know who wouldn't think twice about staying in a hospital with your 3 month-old and your crazed sister and then heading home to an extra 2 year-old on your already full plate. You made it look easy, but I know that it was far from it.

Thank you to my church family: You are truly family, and you stepped up and showed that you really were the arms and legs of the Lord when we needed you. Your generosity and love carried us on the darkest of days. Above all, thank you for your never-ending prayers lifted up on our behalf. The miracles of this story are because of those prayers. We are eternally grateful.

Acknowledgments

Thank you to my friends and extended family: you are a lesson in giving, in creativity, in sacrifice, in love. I would not be who I am today without your investment in my family. Your hours of time, your generous gifts, your encouraging words, and your many prayers: This story would not be what it is without you woven through it. To Billie Kinnaird, Donnave Abt, Megan Yerkes, Chara Weaver, Esther Wegener, Jennifer Dodson, Amy King, Christa Chambers and Sarah Clark: you ladies braved strange and often uncomfortable beds to spend nights with me so that I was never alone. You showed me what it means to represent Christ's love for one's friends.

Thank you to the medical professionals who brought their care and expertise to our case. I changed the names of all the doctors in this story to protect their privacy, but I will never forget their names. I am forever in their debt for the work they did for us and that they continue to do day in and day out for those who would have little hope if it wasn't for them. I am in your debt.

Thank you to my supporters - those of you who did not laugh at the idea that a stay-at-home mom of three young kids could write a book. Those that not only prayed for this book, cheered me on in the days I didn't think I could do it, but also gave financially to the publishing of this book: You stun me with your kindness. I would like to particularly thank these wonderful supporters for their extremely generous financial support: Jim and Donnave Abt, Bethany Brown, Adelaide Green, Steve and Billie Kinnaird, Kevin and Jane Richerson, Karl Tiedemann, Ash and Karissa Thomas, and Kristy Tong.

I am also beyond grateful for the expertise of my editors, Melissa Rea, Esther Wegener, Terri Barnes, and Pencil Edits who not only performed copy edits, but also formatted the publication design of this book. Thank you also to my cover designer at Mulberry Moments, Kristy Tong. You all made me look good.

Notes on twin-to-twin transfusion

If you are currently dealing with twin-to-twin transfusion and have come across my book as a part of your journey, I hope that it will encourage and not scare you. Please know that many who are diagnosed with this syndrome have great success and come away with two healthy babies. Also, we can be thankful that medicine is changing at such a rate that even now the medical advancements in the field of fetal care have improved and changed. Please do not read this book as a how-to in the way of TTT. My only advice to you is to speak up, ask questions, and never, ever be afraid to question something you don't feel is right. Listen to your body. It will not lie. And above all, when your doctors give up, find a new doctor. We have a heavenly Father who does miracles, and I believe He does them through the science of medicine every single day. I mentioned in my thank-yous that I changed the names of my doctors to protect their privacy, but I am always willing to share from my experience. I am always available to answer your questions as best I can, and point you to the places where I found hope. My email is abigail.abt@gmail.com. Please feel free to contact me any time.

Made in the USA
Middletown, DE
04 January 2020

82591314R00104